DYING TO LIVE

DYING TO LIVE

Stories from Refugees on the Road to Freedom

Danielle Vella

ROWMAN & LITTLEFIELD
Lanham • Boulder • New York • London

Published by Rowman & Littlefield
An imprint of The Rowman & Littlefield Publishing Group, Inc.
4501 Forbes Boulevard, Suite 200, Lanham, Maryland 20706
https://rowman.com

6 Tinworth Street, London SE11 5AL, United Kingdom

British Library Cataloguing in Publication Information Available

Library of Congress Control Number: 2019952511

ISBN 9781538118450 (hardcover) | ISBN 9781538118467 (epub)

∞ ™ The paper used in this publication meets the minimum requirements of American National Standard for Information Sciences Permanence of Paper for Printed Library Materials, ANSI/NISO Z39.48-1992.

Cover image: A rescued refugee holds on to a tent on the deck of the Malta-based NGO Migrant Offshore Aid Station (MOAS) ship *Phoenix* as it makes its way to Pozzallo on the island of Sicily, Italy, April 6, 2017.

CONTENTS

PART II: JOURNEY

PREFACE

In this book, I primarily use the term "refugees" rather than "migrants." There are diverse definitions of who qualifies as a refugee in the legal sense of the word. I have opted for the definition of "de facto refugee" offered by the Catholic Church and endorsed by the Jesuit Refugee Service (JRS). This broad understanding of the word "refugee" embraces people who are forced to flee their home country to escape war and armed conflict, persecution, and/or natural disasters, as well as those who are victims of "erroneous economic policy."

ACKNOWLEDGMENTS

Thank you to each and every refugee who shared his or her story with me. Unfortunately not all are featured in this book because I ran out of space. But it was a privilege to listen to every one, and I wish you the very best in your journey to find life. Most of the names used in the stories are fictitious; however, some are the real names, used at the request of the protagonists.

I could only write this book thanks to the logistical and moral support of people working for the Jesuit Refugee Service (JRS) in the places I traveled to meet refugees. I will not name them for fear of leaving someone out. But you know who you are and I am endlessly grateful to you.

JRS is an international Catholic organization with a mission to accompany, serve, and advocate on behalf of refugees and other forcibly displaced persons. Unless otherwise specified, every time reference is made to a nongovernmental organization (NGO), that NGO is JRS and, in the case of Melilla, SJM (Servicio Jesuita a Migrantes). The same applies to the Welcome Network in France. The involvement of JRS in some of these stories gives an indication of the breadth of its mission, from offering legal aid to supporting schools to going on home visits in urban areas to being present in remote refugee camps.

There are a few exceptions. In Belgrade, local Serb NGOs run the two centers I visited and I thank them for their welcome and patience. In Melilla, I thank the sisters of Geum Dodou. And in the United States, specifically in San Diego, the resettlement agency referred to is the International Rescue Committee (IRC). I am indebted to the entire team and volunteers of the IRC in San Diego for their hospitality and enthusiasm to help me with this project. I am also in awe of their amazing work.

Part I

Flight

I

WHERE DO I BEGIN?

Every story has a beginning. When Martin goes back to his, he mentions each member of his family by name, and remembers their home in South Sudan. Holding himself stiffly upright, Martin enunciates each word with deliberation: "I had my father, David; my mother, Mary; my sister, Betty; and my brother, called Paul. My family was not rich but we were happy. In term time, Dad sent me to school in Uganda. Otherwise, Mum and I would go to the farm to work. My dad ran a small business, selling flour and rice, but now I don't know if he lives or not."

Mustafa, a tailor from the city of Raqqa in Syria, dates his family's story to a time when life was beautiful in their country—in his eyes, at least. The father of five says, "School was for free. Everything was cheap. We liked to have children because we didn't have to worry about raising them. Syria was really wonderful." Salma also comes from Syria and she echoes rose-tinted memories of what was. Like Mustafa, she remembers being free from financial worries. "We had a good life. My husband and his brothers worked at a biscuit factory that belonged to the family. We lived in our own house and were paying a bank loan for it." Reminiscing about the family picnics that were a weekly treat, Salma whips out her phone and scrolls until she finds a photo of her home: a terraced house on two floors, gaily painted in pink with a white diamond pattern.

Martin, Mustafa, and Salma are telling the stories of how they became refugees. The way they start reveals just how much they have lost: family, work, dreams, and the simple joy of living. However, not all refugees trace their stories to a nostalgic time. Take Farid, whose life as a taxi driver in Afghanistan was packed with risk and fear every single day. Farid's greatest cause of anxiety was that the Taliban viewed him suspiciously and dogged his every step. One night, a few minutes after he returned home from work, the Taliban knocked at his door and roughly accused him of being a government spy: "If you are not working for the government, from where did you get money to buy a taxi? How can you travel to Kabul without security problems?" Farid was unhappily aware that "in that moment, they could kill me if they wanted and who would ever dare to ask why?"

At some point, Farid decided that enough was enough—he was sure his life was in danger—and he left Afghanistan. In other words, Farid became part of the world's forcibly displaced population of 70.8 million, a statistic so massive that it drowns all those it counts in anonymity and oblivion. And yet each story is exclusive, a unique blend of circumstance, choice, and character. The moment of flight, and the events leading up to that fateful decision, are never the same.

Sometimes life changes from one minute to the next. War explodes in your face. Matthew was nineteen when "the liberation war reached our place" in South Sudan in 1989. The rebels appeared, "very many people, shooting at us." Matthew and the rest of the town dropped everything and ran, with the rebels in furious pursuit. There was only one option: "We had to cross the Nile." People crammed into canoes and paddled frantically with their hands to sweep through the water. Matthew recalls, "We had to force ourselves into that small boat. When we were in the middle of the river, the boat capsized, and so we had to try our level best. One of the children drowned."

Sometimes, the proverbial straw breaks the camel's back: something happens that makes the accumulation of violence, repression, poverty, and total lack of opportunity too hard to bear any longer. Khalid left the Gaza Strip after his family home was demolished: "Death came to our door and we lost our home." Israeli forces bulldozed his neighborhood after Hamas militants fired rockets from there. "We, people from the place, were against this because we knew we'd have problems," says Khalid. "But Hamas said they could do what they liked."

This was the third time his house had been destroyed, and Khalid had neither the energy nor the money nor the will to rebuild it again. The Palestinian man describes life in the crowded territory of the Gaza

Strip as ruined by conflict and corruption. He bitterly criticizes Hamas, the party that rules Gaza, and its running battles with Israeli forces, whose disproportionate actions equal collective punishment. The chronic conflict, coupled with a stiff blockade and infighting between Palestinian factions, has brought the territory to its knees.

When his daughter was born, Khalid itched to take off more than ever. Seeking asylum in Melilla, a Spanish enclave in Morocco, he says, "Why am I here? Because I don't want my daughter to have my experience of war. I want her to have a better life than mine." With an instinctive sense of fairness, he continues indignantly, "I did not choose to be born in Gaza. It is not my fault. We want what everyone else wants, peace and freedom." But it is impossible to be "a peaceful person" in Gaza because everyone is forced to take sides. Ultimately, "a human being means nothing in Gaza."

For Nabeel, it boiled down to an irrepressible desire to live. A refugee from Pakistan who now lives in the United States, Nabeel says, "I left my country because I couldn't live there. I could have survived there all my life; people do. But I say there is a difference between just surviving and living. Animals survive, eat, hunt, do their thing, but living is different."

Once a refugee, life changes forever. Whether the change is for better or for worse depends in good part on the way refugees are treated on their journey and when they reach their destination. But it is not only about hard facts. Each story is also about how those facts are experienced and interpreted. The way we shape our story shows how we make sense of our reality, how we want others to understand it, and how we want them to understand us.

Our story is about our identity, a burning topic for many refugees, because they lose their place in the world when they are uprooted and with it the very sense of who they are. I will never forget what an elderly Sri Lankan man told me about his time in India as a refugee. In his hometown of Mannar, he was a respected civil servant, landowner, and member of the local citizens' committee. He said, "In Mannar, I was someone. As a refugee, I was like all the others."

The stories in this book are told in the words of their protagonists and shaped by what they believe is important to share about themselves, about their country and why they left it, about their journey, and about life in their destination—if they have been fortunate enough to reach it. As Waleed, whom you will meet in these pages, insists, "You need to listen to this voice."

2

DAMNED IF YOU DO OR IF YOU DON'T

EXPECTING THE WORST

Like all of us, Farid never knew what each day would bring, but life in Afghanistan had taught him to expect the worst. More than four decades of conflicts have destroyed this vast country and exacted a deadly toll on its people. For years, the war has pitted the government, backed by international forces, against Islamic insurgent groups, of which the Taliban is the most powerful. At the turn of the century, the Taliban ruled most of Afghanistan by applying a harsh interpretation of Islamic law that drew the world's condemnation. It was ousted by an international coalition in 2001. Since then, Taliban fighters have wrested back control of roughly half of Afghanistan's territory, waging fierce battles, besieging cities and towns, and attacking vital transport routes.

When I meet Farid in Belgrade, the capital of Serbia, he explains how constant insecurity on major roads in Afghanistan made life dangerous for people like him. His job as taxi driver meant he had to transport people from one city and province to another. What's more, the Taliban gave him orders he did not dare disobey, although he knew compliance put him on the wrong side of the law. One time, they asked him to ferry guns in his car. Another time, they turned up at the compound where Farid lived with his wife, children, parents, and other relatives and ordered him to prepare food for twenty "guests" by evening the following day. At the appointed time, they came and disappeared with the food.

Hakeem comes from the same place as Farid, namely the northern province of Baghlan. The Taliban ordered Hakeem's father to join their ranks or to send his son instead. Hakeem's father refused and, shortly afterward, he disappeared while going about his work as a driver. This was three years ago and there has been no sign of him since. "We asked the government to find him, if he is alive or dead, but the government can do nothing in those areas," says Hakeem. He cries when he talks about what happened and the consequences for the family. The combi that Hakeem's father drove for his work did not belong to him. When he disappeared together with the vehicle, the owners callously pursued Hakeem's family for compensation. With their breadwinner gone, the family was in no position to comply.

Hakeem tries to describe what it was like to live between two warring parties: "There were government forces to one side of my village and Taliban forces on the other. Once or twice a month, there were big clashes, and the Taliban used us as human shields." The villagers got caught in more than crossfire. "Every night, the Taliban would send guys with pots to ask for food. If one family gave because they were afraid, their neighbors might give them away to the government forces. Then those who 'supported' Taliban are taken to jail for months." I ask if he knows any people who were taken, and Hakeem replies, "Oh, yes, too many, and their families don't know what happened to them to this day." It is a tough call: "We are afraid of the government and afraid of Taliban too. Whatever we do, one side is going to see us as the enemy." Talk about Hobson's choice.

Farid was uneasily aware that the Taliban viewed him as a potential government spy because his work as a driver took him here and there. Still, he stuck it out until he came face-to-face with a chilling example of what the Taliban did to perceived traitors. Three cousins had come home on vacation from another province in Afghanistan where they worked. The very day they arrived, as the family was enjoying their reunion, the Taliban appeared at the door. They had heard the three visitors worked for the government and had orders to take them for questioning.

Farid's grandfather did his best to dissuade the Taliban, displaying the men's calloused hands to show that they did hard physical labor, not paper pushing in some government office. But the Taliban took them anyway. In the days that followed, Farid's grandfather and other village elders went to the Taliban several times, and each time they received reassurance that the men would be released soon. Farid recalls, "After two weeks, the Taliban threw a paper notice over the wall of our compound, to let us know that if we wanted to recover the bodies, they were in such and such a valley in the mountains."

The callous killing of his cousins was the tipping point for Farid: "I couldn't see more and more of this in the future." He sold his car and his wife's jewelry to pay for an illegal journey to Europe, taking his only son, who was ten years old, and his two brothers. He left his two daughters and wife with his parents, reasonably certain that the Taliban would not harm them.

"WHEREVER YOU GO, WE WILL FIND YOU"

If working as a driver in Afghanistan is a dangerous job, being employed by international forces and enterprises is all the more so. The insurgents brand the people holding such jobs as traitors and give them short shrift if they catch them. Not all those killed for holding such jobs actually do have them—mere suspicion can be enough to snuff out someone's life, which is what happened to the cousins of Farid.

As a truck driver with NATO forces, Zahid's work was doubly dangerous. Zahid came under fire—literally—on a regular basis, "more than a thousand times," he assured me. "We'd travel in a convoy on the road, a line of trucks under escort. The Taliban could attack anytime. The main thing was not to stop. That was the very first thing the army taught us: don't be afraid, just keep moving." An added danger was that the insurgents tried to coerce Zahid's cooperation: "The Taliban tried to force me to give information, like what NATO carried in their convoys, when they would enter and leave the base, and so on. Once, they asked me to load some explosives and to detonate them in the base."

When Zahid flatly refused, the Taliban threatened him. "They told me, you have family, you have children, and you have to think about them too." They abducted, blindfold, and beat him, pushing him into a fan that sliced into his back. He pauses in his narrative to show the deep scars and says he begged his captors for time to decide. "They gave me three days and let me go. I went to hospital to have my wounds seen to. From there I went straight to Pakistan with my family."

Zahid rented a house in Peshawar and felt relatively safe. But after three months, he found in his garden one of the dreaded notes that the Taliban typically uses to communicate. The message was clear: "Wherever you escape to, we will find you." Shaken, Zahid decided to go to Europe, after first installing his wife and children in another location in Pakistan.

Allow me to share one more story in this vein, of an Afghani university student called Hussein, who contacted the police to let them know that the Taliban had planted a bomb on the road just outside his family's house. Hussein was home on vacation from university when he saw them and knew the bomb was intended for army vehicles that would pass by later. Once the police detonated it, the Taliban quickly discovered who was to blame. The threats started soon afterward. Hussein says, "My brother went out of the front door and found an envelope with a handwritten note that someone had left the night before. They accused me of being an agent of the government and an agent of America." The Taliban informed Hussein that he was as good as dead, that they would capture and behead him. Phone calls followed. Hussein says his grandfather advised him to leave the country and gave him the money to do so.

Hussein obeyed, leaving his family and his law course at Nangarhar University in the city of Jalalabad. When I meet Hussein in Belgrade, and he remembers what he left behind to head for an unknown fate, he says he was unlucky. Hussein might have been unlucky, but what happened to him was also the direct consequence of his actions. He made a choice. Why did he take the risk of informing the police? He could at least guess what would happen if he did. Hussein replies indignantly, "I saw the Taliban planting the bomb. Bombs kill innocent people. So I called the government because of this. I did it for myself, for my family, for my country. If I kept quiet, it might have killed my brothers, my sisters, my relatives."

Since 2001, thousands of civilians have been killed in the war of attrition between the insurgency on one side and government and international forces on the other. In addition to being caught in indiscriminate crossfire, civilians are deliberately targeted by insurgents whose favored weapons are suicide attacks, roadside bombs, and other kinds of explosives. The year 2018 proved to be the deadliest on record for civilians in this war, with more than 3,800 killed, per United Nations (UN) estimates. The Taliban emerged as the biggest perpetrator, followed by a domestic version of the Islamic State (ISIS). The government and international forces also pushed up the death toll, with intensified air strikes claiming the highest number of civilian victims ever in 2018. What's more, the government is accused of not doing nearly enough to stop human rights abuses by its own forces.

Apart from the war, Afghanistan suffers from chronic failures in governance, ranking as one of the most corrupt countries in the world. More than half of its people live below the national poverty line. Hussein believes that his country is where it is—in the doldrums—because "we don't have any idea of each person as a human being with rights." He says this is the biggest problem and adds, "The leaders don't think about innocent or poor people but about their own ambition."

3

PAYING THE PRICE FOR PRINCIPLES

"SEND CHRISTIAN CHILDREN AWAY"

As Hussein discovered, abiding by your principles can cost you dearly. Anwar learned the same lesson in Pakistan when he set up his Bright Future School. When we meet in Europe, Anwar becomes enthusiastic at the mere memory of his dream come true: "There were Muslim and Christian children in my school, all studying together. We had three hundred pupils, and we welcomed those who were poor as well as those whose parents could afford to pay, because everyone is equal. It was fifty-fifty." Anwar was doing well. Fields filled with fruit trees surrounded his house and he owned four horses he loved.

Anwar felt fine until, one day, he got a phone call from a certain Abdullah asking him why Christian children were studying in his school. "He told me I must send the Christian children away." Anwar had reason to fear Abdullah, whom he knew by reputation as a "famous and powerful" member of the Pakistani Taliban. He also knew that the Taliban and suchlike groups were capable of making good on their threats because they had attacked hundreds of schools, teachers, and even students. Victims included institutions and individuals that acted in a way condemned by extremists as contrary to Islam—for example, by promoting girls' education. Remember Malala Yousafzai, the youngest Nobel laureate, who was gunned down in northwest Pakistan after speaking in favor of girls' education? She was only fifteen years old at the time.

However, instead of fearing Abdullah, Anwar tried to reason with him: "I told him that Christian and Muslim children are the same." Years later, telling me about that phone call, Anwar spreads his hands in a gesture as if to ask, "What's wrong?" He says, "I didn't see what the problem was. I, Christian, you, Muslim, but you are my sister and we have one God. So why should I be afraid and say this one, yes, and this one, no?" Speaking in rudimentary English, his message comes across perhaps all the more strongly for that: "I wasn't afraid because my school was good."

Abdullah thought different. "He telephoned me again some days later and threatened to set fire to my school if I didn't close it," Anwar recalls. And yet Anwar refused to give in. Then he was woken by some-one banging on the door in the middle of the night to tell him that his school was on fire. With two friends, he rushed over and saw that the desks had been dragged outside and set ablaze. For hours, they strug-gled to put out the flames. Anwar reported everything to the police but they did nothing. "They were afraid," he says simply.

Anwar himself was not afraid—yet. He reopened his school. Two weeks later, as he was sitting at home with his wife and their four children, Anwar heard shooting just outside. What happened next still makes him sad. "My dog ran out as soon as he heard them firing. They shot him in the neck and killed him. He was beautiful, a German shep-herd called Tiger." Barely an hour later, Abdullah called him and went straight to the point: "This time, we didn't kill you. The next time we come, we will kill you all." Anwar was afraid now. The very next morn-ing at dawn, he asked a close friend to call for him and his family. "We went far away to a city near Islamabad. In my place, they didn't know where we had gone," he says. The family stayed indoors from then onward. Anwar did not even allow his children to go to school.

You can run, but you can't hide, not if you don't run far enough. Anwar was driving a motorbike with his friend riding pillion when three people walked into the middle of the road and held up their hands to signal Anwar to stop. "I slowed down. I didn't immediately understand or know who they were," he recounts. In a split second, he saw guns and tried to accelerate. "One bullet came here"—he touches his head behind the right ear—"and my friend was shot in the back." Anwar survived but his friend did not. "He was my close friend," he says with a deep sigh. "Yes, he was like my brother."

Anwar headed for Europe straight away. His wife's earrings and bracelets raised ten thousand euros, of which he paid a smuggler eight thousand for the clandestine journey. He left the rest of the money with his wife "so that my children would be able to eat."

"TRUTH HAS A PRICE"

Countless people have become refugees because they stood up, peacefully, for what they thought was right. Those I have met are usually unassuming in their bravery and unrepentant in their stance. Adil is a man in his late twenties who fled his country, Morocco, to evade certain arrest by police for participating in and reporting about peaceful street protests. His experience as a refugee in Melilla, Spain, has been miserable. No matter: his head is bloody but unbowed. Looking me squarely in the eye, he says defiantly, "I don't regret anything I did. If I had to do it again, I would. Why should we be afraid of calling for our rights? Someone must talk, because if we stay silent, nothing will change."

It all started with the utterly awful and avoidable death of a fishmonger named Mouhcine Fikri in Morocco's northern city of al-Hoceima in October 2016. Fikri was crushed to death inside a rubbish truck when he made a desperate attempt to recover swordfish that had been confiscated by the authorities. Someone switched on the mechanism of the truck's crusher while Fikri was inside. Onlookers said it was the police, but law enforcement authorities denied the accusation. Adil witnessed part of the gruesome scene. "That day, I had gone to the airport to pick up a relative from Holland. We had dinner and they wanted to go out for a walk. I remember, I wanted to sleep because I had work the next day," he says. "Suddenly we saw many people and heard shouting." Adil reached the scene in time to see Fikri's mangled body.

Shocked beyond belief, Adil threw himself heart and soul into the massive street protests that followed Fikri's death, which soon morphed into a social movement highlighting poor socioeconomic conditions in Morocco's northern Rif region. For the Hirak movement, as it came to be known, the unfortunate fishmonger came to symbolize years of structural injustice and neglect suffered by the Rif at the hands of Morocco's rulers. For Adil, Fikri's killing was a personal catalyst that prompted him to act on a situation that already worried him as a "Rifan." He elaborates: "I want my region to be like the other regions of Morocco with hospitals, universities, and employment. The Rif is neglected. We want to be in a position not to have to fight for these rights but to enjoy them already."

Adil insists that the Hirak protests were peaceful: "We did not want to do anything other than to call for our rights." He filmed the protests and uploaded the footage to a website and a Facebook page that he set up with two friends. The reason why: "We decided to write to show the truth to people so that they would know what was really going on." Their social media efforts soon drew tens of thousands of hits and likes.

Although the Moroccan authorities initially tolerated the Hirak protests, the police cracked down in mid-2017, arresting at least 450 activists. Adil started to feel the heat. Once, he was driving a leader of the Hirak movement to a mountain village to meet people there. Two other cars appeared on the lonely mountain road and tried to push Adil's car over the edge, which gave way to a sheer drop. Adil recalls, "I managed to keep to the road and drove to the first place where there were other cars and people. Then those cars disappeared."

Dozens of activists were convicted during trials condemned as unfair by international watchdogs. In a mass trial, a Casablanca court sentenced fifty-three defendants to prison terms ranging from one to twenty years. These sentences were handed down despite credible claims that confessions had been obtained through torture and coercion. The king of Morocco eventually pardoned a few activists but none of the Hirak leaders. Once the arrests started, Adil knew it was only a matter of time. "Every time they arrested someone else, we knew our turn would come," he explains. Before long, his friends were arrested, and he received a police summons to go for interrogation. By then, Adil was in hiding, and a relative crept out at night to give him the news. He says, "I could no longer stay. My only solution was to leave."

Adil departed from Morocco with only the clothes he was wearing, a small bag containing his phone and identification papers, and some money. He left behind his family, his friends, his home, his job, and his car—mentioned in this order. Adil did it for the sake of a truth he badly wanted to tell and accepts the life-changing penalty. His last words in the interview are these: "My grandfather used to tell me that if you tell the truth, you pay a price. Truth has a price."

A MATTER OF FAITH

For Tigiste, it was a matter of faith. She was thrown into prison in her native Eritrea, a small country bordering the Red Sea in the Horn of Africa, for spreading the truth according to her Pentecostal faith. She was fifteen years old at the time. Her religion is important to her not only for its own sake, but also because her adored father was a Pentecostal pastor, on fire to preach the gospel on the streets to all who cared to listen, and even to those who didn't. Tigiste remembers, "Once, he was severely beaten when he was preaching. My mother was crying and he had to stay in bed for a month to recover. But he started to preach again when he got up."

Tigiste's childhood was precarious, torn apart by war, and she clung to her father as a rock. In 2000, her family was ignominiously shuttled out of Ethiopia, after living there for seven years, and back to Eritrea. They were not alone: Ethiopia summarily deported up to seventy-five thousand people of Eritrean origin between 1998 and 2000 because the two countries were locked in a terrible border war. Tigiste's family was given just five days to leave their home in Addis Ababa. Tigiste was only eleven. She says, "The Ethiopian government decided we should go out of this country. That was a bad thing for our life because we built something to live, and to break something is too hard. One night the police came with a bus that goes directly to Eritrea. We spent almost three days traveling, two days in the bus and one day rest, until the border."

The story of Tigiste is long and woeful, and this is only the start. She tells it patiently and in great detail. Back in Eritrea, the family rented a small wooden house in Campo Sudan, a settlement that the government set up for deportees in the port city of Assab. For little Tigiste, whose only memories were of school, friends, and home in Addis Ababa, it was a terrible blow. "It was so hard; you leave everything and go with nothing. I didn't know how to start. I didn't know what I have to do."

Tigiste plunged into a depression and took to her bed for more than a year, missing out on school. Her frail mother was unable to do much for her only child. Tigiste says it was her father who saved her. "I have a good Christian father; I learned so much with him. When I returned to Eritrea, I had bad headaches. I didn't speak. I didn't go out. My mum cry too much and my father . . . he prayed." Tigiste's eyes shine when she remembers her dad. She mimes how he used to carry her in his arms because "my legs, my hands couldn't move."

Tigiste recovered and enthusiastically joined her father in his evangelization drive. By then, he was a full-time Pentecostal pastor and dependent on the goodwill of others for food and other essentials. Tigiste says matter-of-factly, "I started to preach what my God did for me because he saved me when I was sick. This was a good thing for me and I was happy to go out and talk about my God. It was my way of serving God and thanking him."

Tigiste followed her father everywhere he went, even when he was imprisoned for preaching his faith. In 2002, the Eritrean government outlawed all religions except Sunni Islam, Eritrean Orthodoxy, Roman Catholicism, and Lutheran Protestantism. The Pentecostal strain of Protestantism was not on the list, at least partly because it opposes national conscription. In Eritrea, high-school students are conscripted into "national service" without a defined time limit. This is only one of the bizarre dictates of the reclusive and repressive leader, Isaias Afwerki. Nearly half a million Eritreans live in exile around the world. Most left their country to get away from indefinite conscription and other massive violations of human rights. Elections are never held in Eritrea, and the constitution has never been implemented. Political parties, NGOs, and independent media are forbidden.

Even after their religion was banned and their church was closed, father and daughter continued to practice their faith, going house to house. The government warned them but they persisted. "We couldn't stop because we got something from God," explains Tigiste. She harks back to the deportation journey: "We traveled too much. Some people died on the road, but we survived. Sometimes, my mum was sick and, when we prayed, she was better. I gained health. Why did we have to be stopped from preaching?" Why, indeed?

One day, when two neighbors were at Tigiste's house for a prayer service, there was a loud banging on the door. Tigiste went to answer and found ten policemen on the doorstep. They packed the Bibles they found into cardboard boxes, piled everyone present in a pickup truck, and took them to the police station. An officer asked why they insisted on practicing their religion. "He told us they didn't like it that we said war is not good and preached to people not to go to the military," recalls

Tigiste. As she remembers the interrogation after all these years, her voice and expression are adamant: "I am sorry, but God did not say war. We need peaceful things for our country, not war." Tigiste and her father were thrown into prison. "There was no court, no trial. They said, 'We told you two times and you did not stop, so you go to jail now.'" The last time she saw her father was when they were separated to go to different sections of the prison.

Tigiste's mother was released. She confined herself to the family home and died soon afterward. "When I was in prison, I heard my mother had died," says Tigiste, with tears in her eyes. "She was lonely, she was so, so sick, and she died." For nearly two years, Tigiste was imprisoned with another four women in a tiny, dank, and dark cell. She was constantly hungry and felt she would have greeted death as a welcome friend. One day a military officer, one of the prison guards, summoned her to his office. She describes him as a balding man between forty and fifty years of age who wore a necklace made of black wood. Tigiste went eagerly before him, daring to hope that she might be released. Instead, the man raped her.

A sickening routine started. The officer sent for her day after day, and those who shared her cell realized what was going on and mocked her. "Everyone told me, 'You are Christian, but you do these things.' They think I did it because I needed it, but they didn't understand what was happening." Today, when Tigiste tells how she was raped daily as a minor, it is as if she somehow needs to defend herself for being the victim of a crime. She declares that she was weak and innocent, that she "didn't know things," and that what happened destroyed her. Eventually, the officer took Tigiste out of prison and placed her under lock and key in a house in the nearby town, "just like a small prison for me," she says bitterly. "Whenever he needed, he came, raped me, and left, just like a slave."

Another year passed, and still more might have, had the prison authorities not realized that Tigiste was missing when they did a head count of the inmates. Risking exposure, the officer declared that Tigiste had escaped and quickly arranged to have her bundled out of the country. He threatened to kill her if she ever returned. Sensing only that she was about to be free, Tigiste grabbed the opportunity: "I didn't know where I had to go, and I didn't care, but I needed to be out of this place." Before long, Tigiste was alone at the border between Eritrea

and Sudan, at the mercy of the human smugglers and traffickers who
proliferate there.

4

"I AM GOING WHERE I WILL BE FREE"

"THEY WERE WRONG MEN"

At the other end of the spectrum, there are people who escape from their country because they are forced to do terrible things that completely go against who they are. This is the tragedy of Martin from South Sudan. Try as he might to start a new life in Uganda, he carries shame in his heart, like the proverbial albatross around one's neck, and there is no shaking it off. Martin's broken fate is so far from the hopes he once had for his future. He used to dream of being a lawyer, and his father had promised to do everything he could to help him reach this goal.

But that was in the good old days, when Martin's family was happy, in spite of the war that raged in South Sudan. Bitter political rivalry between the country's top leaders had badly deepened ethnic divisions and, in 2013, ignited a civil war that claimed an estimated four hundred thousand lives in five years. Mass killings, plunder, rape, and starvation became the order of the day in the world's youngest nation, only two years after it became independent. The country's rapid decline was all the more pitiful given the universal rejoicing that had greeted its birth. On that day, 9 July 2011, hopes ran high that South Sudan was done with war at last, after fighting long and hard to win its independence from Sudan.

One night in 2016, when Martin was seventeen years old, his family was at home while gunshots rattled all around them outside. Since they lived close to army barracks, they were used to the sounds of war. Suddenly, some thirty armed men appeared at their home. Martin says tersely, "One man attempted to rape my sister in front of all of us. My mum insisted and that was when my mum got shot. She accepted to be killed." Martin's thirty-six-year-old mother did not hesitate: she died to prevent the violation of her daughter. Ironically, when the men turned up and ordered them to go outside, the family was relieved at first. Martin explains why: "They were wearing the uniform of the army of South Sudan, so we thought maybe they were coming to our rescue. That's why, they asked to come outside, and we came. But what they did was different. They killed my mum and that is when I knew they were wrong men."

Martin tries to tell the story of his family's destruction dispassionately, but all the emotion he attempts to control is naked in his eyes. The expression "doe-like" might be a good way to describe them: beautiful and at once wary and trusting. Not that his eyes meet mine at any time. Martin stares over my shoulder at some fixed and invisible point, seemingly oblivious to my presence unless I speak. His words spill out with suppressed intensity.

"They were shooting guns in the air. My sister and my mum were made to sit down and they held my father and me. They asked my father for money but he said he never kept any in the house. All we had was some bread that we ate with sauce we cooked. That is what we stored and my father gave it to them, but . . ." The humble offering did not appease their assailants. Still, they showed an ounce of mercy. "When they shot my mum, my sister was crying. They let her go; they told her to run. We were pulled away, my dad and me. They took us. We left my little brother alone, at the door, crying." Martin's brother was no more than five years old at the time.

As he goes on with his story, Martin continually circles back to his family. He misses them so much and grieves the circumstances in which he lost them. "My mother died in my face. When she was dying, she tried talking to me, but blood was coming from her mouth. She died with open eyes, looking at me." Martin held her in his arms at that moment.

Martin says he does not know the identity of the group that attacked his family but he suspects the army uniform was just a blind. This is hardly surprising. The Sudan People's Liberation Army (SPLA), which had fought for independence, split when South Sudan's president and vice president turned on each other. The latter led a splinter group that became known as the SPLA in Opposition (SPLA–IO), which also suffered many defections. The number of rebel groups mushroomed.

"PLEASE DON'T HOLD THE GUN"

Whoever his captors were, they separated Martin from his father, and the two have not seen each other since that day. Martin goes on wearily, "My eyes were tied, and we moved in the bush all day, without water or food. We were about fifteen in all. One man never wanted to walk; he was shot dead in front of us." They also killed a woman as "an example," to show that those who were reluctant to keep walking would be killed in exactly the same way. Eventually, they reached what Martin describes as a big camp. He was taken to a section for children, which was the most closely guarded: "We could not escape and they always kept their eyes on us."

Now comes the part of Martin's story that is utterly unbearable to him. He sits ramrod straight in his chair, his slim frame standing to attention, and blurts out, "I am sorry to say I learned to shoot a gun." And then, "I am sorry to say I killed a man." Tears fill his eyes again. "I was in the camp for four days, that was when they started teaching us about guns, how to remove all the parts of the gun, how to fix them all. They taught us that fast and they taught us how to shoot." Martin hesitates before getting the dreaded words out: after learning to shoot at a scarecrow, "the last thing we did was shooting a real human."

At first, Martin refused to obey. "I was caned—I have scars all over my back—because I didn't want to shoot. I stayed for days without eating. I had no strength. I could not even stand on my feet. So, I accepted. Then I was fed." More silence. "I accepted to shoot. My eyes were tied. The man I was going to shoot told me, 'Please don't hold the gun.' But they were at my back, and they were going to shoot me if I did not. After shooting, when they opened my eyes, all I could see was the dead body. He was in a T-shirt of the army. He was a child, a man-child." Thin streams of tears spill silently down Martin's cheeks, and he allows them to reach his jaw before wiping his hands over his face and pressing his eyes fiercely with his palms. He looks much younger than his twenty years.

After this "training," Martin was taken to another camp. He does not say much about it, except to describe the leader, the only one in uniform: "He had a beard, he was tall, and they all respected him. He had his personal guards and moved about in a car." Martin was given a role: he was forced to stand at the roadside to flag down passing cars. "We'd give them a signal to stop and then others robbed the cars. They would off-load and take everything."

ESCAPE

It was thanks to this distasteful task that Martin eventually got away. This is where James comes into the story—James, who begged Martin not to forget him, ever. The two became close friends in the camp. Martin says, "James helped me out. We met in the camp. He was already there and fully trained, but he liked me. He was even younger than I was but very sharp. He told me he never wanted to lose me and that I should always remember him as a friend." The two boys planned to try to escape together. One day, when they were at the roadside, they dropped their guns and ran. Martin was faster. "At my back, James was shot dead. He cried my name loud and told me to run. Then he . . ."

Martin leaves the sentence unfinished and instead starts to explain how he managed to leave South Sudan. He ran and ran until he met some passing lorries. "There were army men wearing the Ugandan uniform. They first attempted to shoot me, because I looked strange, and then one man stopped and told me to put up my hands and to kneel. He asked me where I was going and I said, 'I am going where I will be free.' They interrogated me, but still he had a good heart." The soldiers gave Martin a lift to a nearby town called Nimule, unknown to him. For Martin, this was not far enough from the captivity he had just escaped. He crossed the border into Uganda and became a refugee.

Martin has been unlucky in his life so far. The ordeal he described in such detail was the second time that rebels snatched him. The first time, rebels abducted Martin when he was eight years old and made him work as a porter, during the "liberation war" that won South Sudan its independence. That lasted a year, and Martin mentions it only fleetingly, saying his father had searched high and low to get him back. The forced recruitment of children by armed groups is a widespread scourge in South Sudan. According to the estimate of one international organization, government and opposition-affiliated forces have recruited more than nineteen thousand since the start of the conflict in 2013.

Globally, the number of children used in armed conflict has more than doubled in recent years, with almost thirty thousand verified cases, the tip of the iceberg. Boys and girls are routinely used as fighters, at checkpoints, as informants, to loot villages, and as domestic and sexual slaves.

When he has run through his story, Martin loops back randomly to some episodes, perhaps because he wants to make sure I get the picture. Suddenly, he gives a passionate recap of his time as a forced conscript: "I moved without sandals on my feet; I was barefooted. I didn't have a T-shirt. I lived in my sportswear for six months without washing it. We were not even given the chance to bathe; the only chance was when we crossed a small river, that is when the water touches you, or when it rains. I've seen people dying when they got tired; they cannot walk anymore. I've seen people killed before my eyes, people slaughtered like goats. We were forced to watch how they were killed. That was the training they were giving us." Despite the training he was given, and the atrocity he was forced to commit, Martin remains a good and gentle young man. The biggest tragedy is that his belief in this essential goodness in himself has been destroyed.

5

"I WAS ALREADY DEAD"

A BOY WITH A DIFFICULT LIFE

Daoud describes himself as a "boy with a difficult life." When he was five, his parents died and left him in the care of the man he came to look upon as his father. They worked together from the time Daoud was ten, "lifting stones out of a mine" in Western Sahara. Western Sahara is located on the northwest coast of Africa and bordered by Morocco, Mauritania, and Algeria. Formerly a Spanish colony, the territory has been fought over by its native Sahrawi people and Morocco for more than forty-five years. Today, a Sahrawi movement called the Polisario Front controls 20 percent of the territory and runs a self-declared Sahrawi Arab Democratic Republic, while Morocco occupies the lion's share in terms of land and natural resources. Morocco has built a long desert wall, surpassed in length only by China's Great Wall, to separate the two sides. More than 170,000 Sahrawi refugees live just across the border in Algeria, in remote camps in the Sahara Desert. Human rights agencies say that Morocco systematically prevents gatherings aimed at promoting self-determination in Western Sahara.

So much for the bigger geographical and political picture, about which Daoud volunteers no information. What he tells is his own story: that one day a part of the mine where he worked collapsed and crushed the man he knew as his father. "The mine chief buried him, I don't even know where," says Daoud. To this day, it bothers him that he does not know where the grave is. Daoud continued working at the mine, but

"Polisario used to come to warn us that we had to leave, because we had no right to work in this territory." After several warnings, Polisario came and forced the miners out at gunpoint. Daoud and some others crossed the border into Mauritania and found work slaughtering camels for their meat. After a bit, he went to Algeria.

This turned out to be a disastrous move because Daoud was kidnapped by what he describes as a "mafia" in the border region where Algeria meets Mauritania and Western Sahara. He does not know much about the identity of his abductors, only that they "did lots of smuggling of different goods and weapons" and treated him like a brute beast of burden for three years. Smuggling between Morocco and Algeria is a modern version of cross-border trading practices that are centuries old. A wide selection of goods is smuggled from one country to the other, destined for both the local market and farther afield. The goings-on range from relatively innocuous, such as the smuggling of clothes, food, cigarettes, and subsidized fuel, to highly illicit, such as the trafficking of weapons, drugs, and, one of the most lucrative "commodities" of all, migrants. While many networks consist of local concerns run by so-called barons and are rooted in age-old tribal and family links that connect one side of the border to the other, transnational criminal elements are also increasingly active.

Whichever of these outfits grabbed Daoud, he had a miserable life for all the years he was confined in forced labor camps. Daoud describes his life in a soft-spoken and dignified way, his sad eyes looking straight at me. While he might be vague about other details, Daoud is strikingly articulate about what it felt like to be a virtual slave: "We were never paid, just fed once a day, and very bad food at that. The same clothes we had for working were those for sleeping, always dirty. We didn't cut our hair or even wash at times. I'd want to wash, but we had to hurry, because they came for us to go to work." Daoud was woken up at three or four every morning. "I got used to it, working from then to nighttime," he says. Most of his backbreaking work consisted of digging wells with an axe in the desert. "My hands were always injured."

In one incident that still rankles, one of Daoud's abductors kicked him viciously for perceived disobedience. "My side still hurts, and when I feel it I instantly remember my past, all my life, what happened to me," he says, touching the place where the kick landed. Next, he gestures to his forehead to show an ugly scar. His explanation shocks Farah, the translator. Wide-eyed, she turns to me and exclaims, "Look at this! They marked him like a beast, like a cow, because he was a slave." Daoud says there were others who were marked on different parts of their face to distinguish which camp they came from: "They mark with burning metal, the same method, in different places." Farah unconsciously mimics Daoud's gestures on her own forehead and side. "Unbelievable," she repeats, shaking her head in visible distress, "marked on his forehead and everything!"

At first, Daoud did not seriously entertain thoughts of running away because "even if I did manage to escape, there was nowhere to hide, only desert." Then, after about three years, he suddenly changed his mind. Farah asks, "Why did you decide to leave? Was it because of the mark on your forehead or the kick?" He replies that it was neither. "One day, I woke up and said to myself, 'I can't continue like this; it's either death or escape.' On that very day, I told my friends, 'I'm leaving or else I'll commit suicide.'" Daoud's reasoning was simple but profound: "What did I have to lose? My life? I had no life. I was already dead. So, if I tried to escape and they killed me, I wouldn't lose anything. As a slave, I was not alive. Dying and staying were the same thing, so I had to escape. It was impossible to live as a human being like that."

At sunset, after the day's work, Daoud waited until the guard's back was turned and jumped out of the back of the pickup truck, hidden by the sand scattered by the turning wheels. Daoud recalls, "I rolled over and, when I looked up from the ground, I saw a Bedouin who asked me where I had come from. I asked him to help me and he told me I must leave immediately because they'd find me." This is how Daoud took to the road. He was determined to escape and to find a life better than the misery he had known so far. He says, "Since I was born, I don't have a life like other people. I have known only suffering. I lost my parents, I worked in a mine, and I was a slave. From the moment I opened my eyes to the world, I have been working. I never went to school. I am twenty-five and, so far, I haven't had a life."

"I FELT I HAD NO VALUE"

Ten-year-old Habib was snatched from his nomadic parents by a man who gave him candy that drugged him. Habib used to go with other children to seek out French tourists who came on quads to the desert. One day, "somebody gave us sweets," he recalls. "We ate them and fell asleep. When we woke up, we found ourselves in Tindouf, with many other children who had been kidnapped before us. Some we knew; others we didn't know."

This is how Habib starts his story. He was kept for an eternity of fifteen years in captivity. First, he was imprisoned in Tindouf, Algeria, where Polisario is headquartered, close to the borders of Western Sahara, Mauritania, and Morocco. "You can't escape," he says. "In the forced labor camps, they know everyone, and they recognize your camp from the clothes you wear. If you leave, you are a dead man." Habib was put to work in underground mineral mines, where "we worked all day, without stopping, until darkness fell and we could no longer continue."

Like Daoud, Habib gives a striking picture of what it was like: "They treated us like objects, machines. If you refused to work, you were left without meals, and sometimes locked up too. Did they beat us? Oh, you don't need to ask that. The answer is, all the time!" He laughs resentfully. "When you work, there is always someone smoking and watching. You have a set time to finish the work, and if you don't finish on time, you are punished. If you don't go on time, you are punished."

What hurt Habib more than the forced labor and the beatings was the sure knowledge that he had no value in anyone's eyes. The realization hit him most forcefully when he was badly injured at the age of sixteen. Habib was climbing down into a mine with a rope that frayed and tore, causing him to fall nine meters (thirty feet). The fall broke his leg. All the camp leader did was fashion a makeshift splint and bandage and leave him like that. Habib tried to heal the scratches and bruises on his face by dabbing detergent powder on them. He was immobilized for months, during which time the only help he got was from a woman who looked after the children in the work camp. She used to clean his wounds from time to time and feed him. The others were afraid to help him for fear of being punished. Another time, Habib broke his tooth and cut his face. Once again, "they left me to one side; no one looked after me. I felt like I have no value. I could get sick. I could get hurt. I could die—it wouldn't be any of their business."

After eleven years of this life, Habib was transferred by the network that "owned" him to another work camp near Ramlia, in Morocco. This place was slightly better because the boys got pocket money sometimes.

However, they were still virtually prisoners and not allowed to go any-where except to work. This time, they were involved in fuel smuggling across the border between Algeria and Morocco, an endemic practice because of the huge difference in price from one side to the other, with Algeria being much cheaper.

Habib's chance to escape came when he was ordered to go and search for water. He walked and ran all day, until he reached Ramlia, not daring to rest for fear of being caught. Like Daoud, he had no identification papers of any kind and was likely to get into trouble for this sooner or later. He tried to tell his story to the authorities but they disbelieved him. So he journeyed on with a clear goal: "I wanted to have my own life and to find out what happened to my parents."

6

"ALL I COULD DO WAS PRAY"

ESCAPING ISIS

Eighty lashes: this was the punishment inflicted on Mustafa because ISIS found an unaccompanied woman in his shop. Mustafa, who used to love life in Syria so much, started to hate it once ISIS took over Raqqa, the city where he had always lived. His work as a tailor of women's clothes became very difficult because women were forbidden from meeting men without their husband or brother present.

The Islamic State hardly needs introduction. Of all the fundamentalist terrorist groups on the global scene, it easily ranks among the most notorious. ISIS won its reputation with acts of extreme barbarity calculated to strike terror in the hearts of those witnessing them, whether in a public square in Raqqa or around the world in videos disseminated online. ISIS has branched out in several conflict zones, such as Libya and Afghanistan, and its affiliates have carried out deadly terrorist attacks around the world.

Most of all, ISIS has left its mark on the territory where it came into being and once held sway. ISIS was spawned in Iraq from a merger of Al Qaeda—another infamous terrorist outfit—with other Iraqi jihadist groups. It took advantage of the chaos and insecurity in the region, especially the war in neighboring Syria, to mobilize as an ascendant force. At its height, ISIS occupied territory in Iraq and Syria that was roughly equal in size to Great Britain. ISIS ruled by imposing an extreme and distorted interpretation of sharia, using morality police to ensure obedience through terror.

Mustafa was one of their subjects and could not take it. As soon as he could, he left with his family, and they now live as refugees in Beirut, the capital of Lebanon. Over tiny cups of excellent coffee in their living room, Mustafa and his wife explain how desperate they were to leave Raqqa. However, since ISIS forbade anyone from leaving its territory, they could only do so clandestinely and at huge risk. "We tried to leave but we couldn't find a way," Mustafa says earnestly. And no wonder: the couple reel off a list of revolting punishments meted out by ISIS for real or imagined infractions of its repressive rule. There were floggings and crucifixions every day, amputations of hands, sewing of lips, and severing of tongues. Those suspected of smoking had their fingers broken if they smelled of nicotine. A particularly grotesque tactic was to plant the heads of those executed in public places, on the spikes of park railings or lined up on a wall. Mustafa's wife, Asma, says, "Once my daughter saw a head that was so small and she was terribly afraid."

Asma lets her husband do most of the talking. She sits and listens, cradling her youngest child in her arms, and reinforces Mustafa's narrative every so often. Although they are remembering horrors that intimately impacted their family, she remains calm. The worst part of their story is about Mustafa's younger brother, who dared to stand up to ISIS. Mustafa recalls how ISIS "wanted to force us to pray all the time" and how one day his exasperated brother asked them, "Why do you make me pray? I will go to hell if I don't; you will not come with me." Wael was carted off to prison but ISIS said he would be released within days.

Shortly after his brother's arrest, Mustafa took his family out in the car to visit relatives and drove past Wael's lifeless body hanging on a cross in the street. ISIS had shot Wael, crucified him, and left his body hanging there for three days. Mustafa's six-year-old daughter saw him and started screaming hysterically, "Uncle! Uncle!" Seeing her beloved uncle like this was beyond bearing for Fatima. "She was very close to my brother," explains Mustafa. "Wael was like a father to her, and she was closer to him than anyone. He had practically brought her up and he used to take her out to restaurants to treat her and buy her gifts."

As for Mustafa, he mourns the lost years that his twenty-seven-year-old brother will never live. "He was still such a young man. He hadn't seen anything of life yet," he says, a look of profound pity descending on his face. I remark that Wael was a very courageous man. Mustafa replies in angry frustration, "Yes, because he was speaking to people who had no sense at all!" Yet these senseless people were all-powerful in that time and place. Mustafa sighs. "What could I do? I couldn't fight an enemy who does not fear God. All I could do was pray to God and ask him for help."

The fanatical and twisted version of Islam according to ISIS turned the family against their own faith. "We hated the Muslim religion because this treatment made us hate it. This is not Islam; Islam is about love and peace." Much as both Mustafa and Asma loved Raqqa, and reluctant as they were to leave their elderly parents behind, the couple fled at the first opportunity. Asma concludes by saying, "I would never have imagined that I'd leave Syria, that I would ever leave Raqqa. Before, I loved it so much that I never used to go anywhere, not even to Damascus or Aleppo." But now, "after what we saw and what we felt and experienced, we never want to go back."

PAYING A HIGH PRICE FOR FREEDOM

"The more you say, the more you describe, you will never manage to say exactly what happened." I hear this from Zainab, another Syrian who lives as a refugee in Beirut after fleeing from ISIS. When asked, she dutifully describes life under ISIS and her journey to safety, but adds the proviso quoted above. It is not the first time I have heard it. Many refugees assert that they do not have the words to recount what they lived and saw. A Syrian man I met in Croatia in early 2016, when he was on his way to Germany, said, "I'm trying to explain why I left but it's difficult: feeling and meaning, my friend, you know?" Just as he could never fully explain what war was like, I could never fully understand, because I had not been there and because my mind rebels against even imagining the unspeakable.

Nevertheless, Zainab does her best to give a picture of what life under ISIS felt like: "When I remember ISIS, my whole body shakes. It was like being in living death." Her biggest fear was that her ten-year-old son might be kidnapped. "I felt ISIS was looking at my son, and they had just taken one boy who was a year older, and they did not give him back." ISIS used to take boys to join their ranks. Zainab's husband was working in Lebanon, so she conferred with her father-in-law, who shared her misgivings. He told her, "If you don't take him now, they could take him tomorrow." That very night, Zainab's husband started to make arrangements for his family to leave.

What I heard from Mustafa, Zainab, and others who fled ISIS is echoed by a host of sources. Reports record how ISIS declared their intended victims to be heretics to justify the punishments meted out, including the beheading, shooting, and stoning of men, women, and children in public spaces. Hideous as it was, however, this behavior was not the only terror stalking those trapped in ISIS territory. A massive international coalition, joined by seventy-four nations, resolved to destroy ISIS and pummeled its so-called caliphate with air and artillery strikes. Working with Syrian and Iraqi partners who engaged ISIS in battle on the ground, the US-led coalition carried out more than thirty-four thousand strikes in four and a half years. Civilians dreaded the strikes, which were not as discriminate as international forces claimed.

Zainab says her children used to sleep in their clothes and shoes to be ready to run if there was a strike. Asma remembers being at a loss for what to do: "When the bombings started, I didn't know where to put my kids: in the bathroom, in the kitchen, where would be the safest place? That's why I don't want to go back, ever. Twice, the planes dropped bombs really close to our house." Another woman decided to prepare for the worst: "When we lived under ISIS, there was so much bombing. I used to roll the children in blankets and put one in each corner of the room, so that if they were killed, they wouldn't explode into bits. I'd be able to bury them in one piece, in the blanket."

The intense air and ground campaign achieved its aim. Step-by-step, ISIS was driven out of all the territory it once held and, by March 2019, the last pocket in Syria was liberated. That was the end of the caliphate. However, this does not mean the end of ISIS, as its victims are quick to caution. ISIS survives as an insurgency in the region and remains capable of doing considerable harm. Their defeat changes nothing for those who shared their stories with me: they will never return to their homes in former ISIS domains. Apart from the traumatic memories, and the fact that so many people have fled or been killed, the military strikes left devastation in their wake. In just one example, the UN has declared Raqqa "unfit for human habitation" and 70 percent destroyed.

The US-led coalition exacted a high price from civilians to free them from ISIS but is reluctant to acknowledge this. While there is recognition that the strikes killed and injured civilians as well as ISIS fighters, there is a substantial gap between military estimates and those of Iraqis and Syrians who lived through the bombardments. An independent monitoring group called Airwars claimed that a fair estimate of the civilian death toll from coalition actions in Iraq and Syria was between 8,190 and 13,091, compared to the coalition's paltry estimate of "at least 1,335" as of September 2019.

The coalition is certainly not the only offender in this respect. From the start of the conflict, the UN has documented the "flagrant abuse of military power displayed by all parties to the conflict" and remarked that all territorial gains have cost civilians dearly. The Syrian-Russian military alliance has been charged not only with indiscriminate attacks but also with deliberately targeting civilians and using banned munitions such as chemical weapons.

A dizzying array of groups has waged war in Syria since 2011. It is practically impossible to sum up who they are. They have mutated over the years, disbanding and forming new affiliations, fighting new battles as soon as the dust clears from the old. Several countries back one side or the other. The eight years of war have fueled the largest forced displacement since World War II. It is estimated that some twelve million Syrians have been displaced, either within Syria itself or abroad, mostly in neighboring countries, a toll that amounts to more than half of Syria's prewar population.

KILLED FOR NOTHING

Many people left their homes, never to return, when the war arrived on their doorstep. "My daughter kept saying, 'Bomb, bomb, bomb,' until she was three years old," says Hibah, a woman from the northern city of Aleppo. This was after a bomb hit the mosque right behind the apartment block where Hibah lived. "She was a year and a half when it happened. When the shooting and bombing woke us up at night, I was so scared. My husband was sleeping on the balcony because of the heat." What Hibah's husband remembers is that their living room had never seemed so big as it did that night, when he crawled frantically across the floor to reach the relative safety of the bedroom. The couple huddled in a corner with their baby until morning and left home at dawn. "Before, we used to hear the sounds of war in the city, yes, but never so close," says Hibah. "When it happened, my biggest fear was that something would happen to my husband or my daughter, and then what would I do? That's what I kept thinking: 'If something happens to them, what will I do?'"

Safiya, who lived in a neighborhood on the southern outskirts of Damascus called Hajar al-Aswad, tells her story in lurid detail. Hajar al-Aswad was one of the early battlegrounds between Syrian government forces and the Free Syrian Army (FSA), the self-styled "moderate armed opposition" that was formed in 2011 when the regime cracked down on peaceful protests. In 2012, fierce fighting in the thick of the district's residential areas forced some four hundred thousand people to run away in the space of a few days. Safiya was one of them. "One day, the entire neighborhood was bombed," she declares dramatically. "I ran out of our home and suddenly I was stepping on dead bodies in the street. People were calling us to go on vans to leave."

As Safiya was racing to the nearest van, a boy told her she had blood on her sweater. "I thought I was sweating; I didn't realize I was bleeding. I looked down and saw blood. Then I felt the pain." It was a shrapnel wound. Safiya kept running, picking her way through the bodies that seemed to be everywhere, "some still alive. I could see them moving." Safiya's eyes took in microscopic details in those few seconds. She points to her neck, near the collarbone: "One man had been hit here and he was shaking and dying. I saw his soul going out of him."

Then there was the death of Samir, her neighbor's son. Safiya brings back his final moments: "Samir was hit; his mother was crying and holding him as he fell. We were calling her to come to the van; she was crying and screaming. I can't forget this." Safiya pauses a moment and then continues: "Samir was killed for nothing. He was so young, in his early twenties, not a troublemaker or anything, just a very nice boy. Everyone loved him." Until then, Safiya did not really know what war was, although they had all heard the sounds of battle coming ominously closer. "Those bodies on the ground, when I rushed out of the house, were the first I had ever seen. I was shocked, for myself and for my children, who saw it too. I couldn't sleep for ages after that."

The van took Safiya and the others to a school in the nearby Yarmouk district. The school had been turned into a makeshift camp where doctors were available to dress Safiya's wound and where they stayed for a few days, until the food ran out because the vehicle bringing supplies was bombed. Safiya, her husband, and their four children then left and started walking, without any aim other than the vague intent to reach Damascus. She recalls, "I was exhausted and in pain because the sweat was seeping into my wound. My youngest daughter was so tired; we were taking turns to carry her."

When Safiya could take no more, she went to knock at the first door she came across. A couple greeted them. "I had no idea who lived there. I told them my daughter was hungry. They invited us inside, asked us where we had come from and what happened, and gave us food." The hosts had no room to keep the family, but asked their son if he could do so instead. He welcomed Safiya and her family, giving them mats to sleep on, food, and drink. Safiya will be forever grateful: "They took nothing from us, no money. They were so good to us, and when someone does this, you never forget."

After a few weeks, Safiya decided to return home, to check things out. "I found the door of my house wide open and everything broken inside. When I saw my home, I felt really sad. My heart was on fire," she says. Despite the damage, Safiya decided to try to take a shower. She was longing to do so because she had not taken one in weeks. "I went upstairs, wondering what could happen." Safiya found a bit of fuel for the water heater and took her shower. Then, "just as I started to wash my youngest daughter, a bomb hit our neighborhood. Everything shook. I wrapped my daughter in a towel, although she was still covered in soap, and we all ran out." They never returned.

I AM YOU; YOU ARE ME

Salma, whose story started with happy memories of her pink house, the family biscuit factory, and weekly picnics, remembers exactly what she was doing when the fighting reached her door. "I was making tomato sauce for the year, preparing and preserving the tomatoes after setting them out to dry in the sun," Salma begins, and she goes on to explain the preserving process in detail. "Then the shooting started and my father-in-law said we should go to another house. I couldn't bear to leave the sauce behind. So I put it into bottles, although it wasn't ready yet, and I took it with me."

Although street battles between the government and the FSA were being waged practically on their doorstep, Salma and her family were not too worried, because the rebels came from their own place. "They were our relatives, cousins and sons, so we thought it would fizzle out— either the army would put a stop to it or they would come to their senses." Rapidly unfolding events proved them wrong. Although Salma and her family did return home, the rebels evicted them some time afterward. "FSA loudspeakers announced that from ten in the morning to ten in the evening, all homes in the area had to be vacated," says Salma. "They took over our home and turned it into a jail for women on the ground floor and for men on the first floor." She turns to her phone to show me the house as it stands now. Bombardments have sliced it in half, so that one side is gone and the jagged gray edge of exposed concrete rudely interrupts the pink and white diamond pattern on the walls of what remains.

From then on, "I moved a lot," Salma assures me with a small smile. First, her family went to live in a block of flats vacated by others who had fled before them. Then the army bombed the building. Their neighbors, a family of eight women, were eating breakfast when the bomb hit. All were killed. Salma's family moved to another place where they found no shelter except a cowshed. Salma had to scrub it clean for eighteen days before they could move in.

For years, Salma struggled to make do, working all kinds of jobs to earn enough money to keep her family going. There was no denying that life was getting harder than ever. Even so, when her husband suggested that the family go to Lebanon because he had an offer from a biscuit factory there, Salma burst into tears. "I was thinking of staying in Syria, even with all these things," she says. "But my husband insisted."

Of all the episodes Salma shares with me, too many to be recorded here, one that stays with me is how buying bread became deadly because the army used to bomb people queuing outside the bakery. "Sometimes, my children came home with bread spattered with blood," says Salma. Bread was rationed due to desperate food shortages, forcing Salma to resort to subterfuge. "They would give you just four flatbreads, but we had five children. I'd change my clothes and cover my face with my headscarf, so that the baker would not recognize me, and I'd go again to buy more bread. My daughter would go, too, so we could get as much bread as possible."

Salma's story strikes a chord with me, evoking a story that my mother used to tell us about her childhood. My family is Maltese, and the tiny island of Malta was a fiercely contested territory in World War II due to its strategic position in the middle of the Mediterranean Sea, between Europe and North Africa. Since it was a British colony at the time, Axis air strikes flattened much of Malta. The island was also subject to relentless siege warfare. At one time, the daily ration of bread for a family of six was approximately half a loaf, meticulously weighed, and people risked imprisonment just for cutting and taking a thin slice of bread between the two halves.

My mother would set the scene by explaining all this. Then she would tell us about Salvina, a devoted family servant who once took the big risk of bringing home both halves of one loaf. It happened like this: after the baker's wife had served her, the baker called out to Salvina in the street to remind her to pick up the bread, because he did not know she had already taken it. My mother told this story to show us how much they had suffered during the war, and how much Salvina loved her and her siblings, to the extent that she risked prison to give them more to eat that day.

The story of a siege survivor of World War II, a tale more than seventy-five years old, bears distinct resemblance to the story of a siege survivor from Syria a few years back. This sets me thinking. What comes instantly to mind is the time-honored adage *plus ça change, plus c'est la même chose* ("The more things change, the more they remain the same"). I think about how my parents, my grandparents, my uncles and aunts all experienced the fear of air strikes and risked starvation under siege. Even if such horrors seem distant from our lives now, they are not a world apart; they are integral to my family history and not so ancient either. And then, in a lightbulb moment, I remember something I read in the National Museum of Immigration on Ellis Island in New York Harbor: "I am you. You are me. We are us."

Part II

Journey

LEAVING SYRIA BEHIND

UNFORGETTABLE DETAILS

Mariam was thankful to find help cheerfully given on the exhausting journey away from ISIS territory in Syria. She was traveling to Lebanon with her elderly father-in-law and four young children. They left Raqqa with scores of other people, including a bunch of friendly young men who helped the mothers carry their children and their bags. The entire group crept out of the city during the time of evening prayer, when everyone was obliged to attend the mosque, so ISIS would hopefully be unaware of their escape. Mariam says, "Within fifteen minutes, we had to leave the village. No one could make a sound. We ran on tiptoes, carrying the youngest children."

After going part of the way by bus, the refugees walked through the night for about nine hours, until they reached an FSA checkpoint. "We waved white blankets in the air to show them we come in peace," Mariam recalls. She was relieved, especially for her father-in-law, who had nearly collapsed with fatigue just a few minutes before. Everyone sank down gratefully to the floor in a few dilapidated rooms located at the checkpoint, laying their children to rest on mats scattered around the floor. The FSA was checking the families, one at a time.

Suddenly, the group of obliging young men whipped guns out of their backpacks—"We thought they had food and clothes in them," Mariam says—and opened fire on the FSA fighters. Those few seconds are frozen in her memory: "I reached out to get my daughter and put one foot in front of the other. A bullet hit the ground just at my feet. The sand flew into the air. This is what I can't forget: the sand going everywhere. If I hadn't put my foot forward at that very second, I would have been hit." In the chaotic scramble for safety, "everyone was step-ping on everyone else." Mariam crawled on her knees to search for her children, who had fallen asleep on the mats, and panicked when she lost sight of two of them. Within seconds that seemed like a lifetime, she found them.

Mariam and her traveling companions surmised that the young men came from ISIS. Her experience reveals the dangers of the journey facing Syrians who fled their homes and passed through a country carved between warring groups. Mariam made it, and the events she relives seem a world away from the mundane quiet of her rented flat in Beirut, where she is "so happy" because she feels secure. When I re-mark that she has a knack for vividly describing what she went through, so much so that I can picture it, Mariam says, "It was very hard. That's why I remember the details."

It seems her son remembers them too. No more than ten years old, he sits silently next to Mariam on the sofa. When she describes the shootout, he pipes up to say that a nine-year-old boy was shot dead in the fracas. They buried him under the olive trees, and his mum found him before she went back on the bus and she cried. Mariam's son goes on to share another memory from that trip: at the second FSA check-point, a teenage boy was found with a picture of ISIS leader Abu Bakr al-Baghdadi on his phone. This was a fatal discovery: the FSA executed him there and then.

Mariam elaborates: "We went by bus to the next checkpoint, and they searched us again, and this is when they found the boy, he was about fourteen years, with the picture of Baghdadi. They tied his hands behind his back and told him to walk to a sand dune they had created as a shield. Then they shot him dead." Did Mariam actually see this? "Oh, yes, we both did, didn't we?" she says, turning to her son and ruffling his hair. "We were on the bus and it was turning around just as the boy was walking up that hill. By the time the bus reached the road, they had shot him. He was just a boy traveling alone; I sat next to him on the bus. He said he had deleted all the pictures he had of ISIS, but he must have missed this one."

In a country like Syria, ravaged by pervasive conflict, life comes very cheap. One warring party frequently views with misgiving those moving from the territory controlled by another. If the combatants decide that their fears might be justified, mercy appears to be in short supply. Their suspicions are not always groundless, as the shootout proved. But most of the refugees just want to find a safe place, and the mistrust they face on the way is irksome, insulting, and sometimes even dangerous.

Mariam experienced something of this when passing through territory held by Kurdish fighters to get to Damascus. Everyone alighted from the bus at the checkpoint, and the driver was ordered to proceed to the next village and to wait for his passengers there. Some eight hours passed, and those manning the checkpoint did nothing but smoke and drink coffee, leaving the families to wait and wilt in the heat. Mariam's view: "They just wanted to keep us waiting because we are Arabs and they are Kurds." But this was unacceptable to Mariam because her children were hungry and thirsty, and she could see that her baby daughter was very unwell. She recalls, "I had powdered milk but no water to mix it with. I asked for water but they did not give me."

Mariam singled out a tall and broad-shouldered man who looked like he was in charge, wearing sunglasses and with a cigarette dangling out of the corner of his mouth. She dispatched her father-in-law to plead with him. No such luck: "He started shouting and swearing and told my father-in-law to shut up." So Mariam plucked up courage and went herself, carrying the baby in her arms. She told the man, "Our children have not eaten since yesterday. May God be with you; please let us pass." He looked at her closely and barked, "Pass!" The relief comes back to Mariam's face when she remembers that moment. To hear her talk about the village they went to, you would think she had found a five-star hotel, so great was her delight. "We found water and food for the kids, even slides and swings for them to play. We bought sandwiches, we washed, and we made milk for baby."

Once they reached Damascus, Mariam's husband, who was anxiously waiting in Lebanon, arranged the last leg of their journey with a smuggler. They entered Lebanon illegally because it would have been too expensive to do otherwise. At the border, the smuggler instructed them to run from his car toward the mountains, where they found hundreds of people about to cross together.

The trek was tough. "It was not like this," Mariam says, holding her fingers stiff and inclining her straight hand to indicate a slope. "It was like this," and her hand flips to vertical. "We spent two hours going up and down, walking in a line, one in front of the other." A handful of smugglers, wearing wide-brimmed hats to shelter their faces from the blistering sun, accompanied the group. The way down was harder because it was so steep. One of Mariam's sons fell and rolled out of her sight down the slope. A smuggler, whom Mariam estimates was about eighteen years old, reassured her that the boy would be fine. He raced down, picked him up, wiped his face clean, and told Mariam, "See, don't worry. He's OK!"

Meanwhile, Mariam's eldest son kept darting off. She smiles at the memory: "He was not being disciplined because he kept running ahead to see if he could spot his dad. The smuggler ran after him to bring him back to the group." Mariam's husband had been working in Lebanon, and his family had not seen him in two years. She says, "I was motivating the kids to continue walking by telling them that when they went down, they would see their father." Sure enough, her husband was waiting for them on the other side of the mountain, with a car borrowed from a friend. This is a story with a happy ending: "The journey took us one week and one day. We arrived safely and I will never go back."

THE GOOD DRUZE

Mustafa, whose brother was executed by ISIS for daring to question why he should pray, also went from Raqqa to Beirut. But the journey of his family stretched to twenty-two days, the tempo dictated by the war. Despite all he has experienced, Mustafa retains a sense of humor that comes through as he recounts their journey. He tells the story at his own pace and, whenever I ask a question that might preempt the next episode, he tells me with an impatient grin to brace myself for what's coming next.

At the border with Lebanon, the family tried to cross at the official checkpoint, because they had all their papers in order. But the soldier in charge, referred to as a "general" by Mustafa, proved to be unwelcoming: "We waited for about six hours and then the Lebanese army general tore my papers when I presented them." Just as Mariam had done in Syria, Mustafa's wife managed to convince the angry soldier to let them pass. "My wife tried next. She took all our papers and pleaded with him, and he let her through. He told her to bring her husband and then he saw me. He said angrily, 'You again?' But he let us through."

The border crossing capped an eventful three weeks for Mustafa and his family, which he remembers chiefly as a time when they were "sold" every step of the way. "I say 'sold' because we had to keep paying whoever we were transferred to next," he explains. As they were approaching the Druze city of Sweida in southwest Syria, after seven hours in a filthy cattle truck, the family had their ID cards confiscated and were closely questioned. They bought bottles of water "at twenty times the usual price." Next, they were passed onto "another big boss and our IDs went with him." They paid again and set off in one of a group of four cars, toward a Syrian army checkpoint, which they reached in the early morning.

It was at this time that their Good Samaritan appeared, or it might be more fitting to call him a Good Druze. The Druze people are a minority in the Middle East distinguished by their secretive religion, which is an eclectic blend of doctrines, and by their strong cohesion. In Syria, they made up around 3 percent of the prewar population. Not without difficulty, they have managed to maintain precarious neutrality throughout the country's conflict. Mustafa identified the man who suddenly appeared at the checkpoint as a Druze "because he had the hat"—the trademark white hat that Druze men wear. As he drew up in a car, accompanied by another man, they could see he held a big gun. "We felt he was a sheikh," says Mustafa, using an Arabic title of respect for a venerable man. The man told the soldiers at the checkpoint, "These people are under my umbrella; they are safe with me." The soldiers made no attempt to stop him. He beckoned to the four cars to follow him and told Mustafa and the others, "When you are with me, there is no need to be scared."

When their awe-inspiring and mysterious benefactor appeared, their driver told Mustafa's family, "God wants to protect you: this man is like a bird sent from the sky for you." Mustafa never learned this man's name or anything about him other than "he has a very powerful word around those parts, and is very much respected. He is known to be a good man; he does not like to harm others and wants to help." The Druze man escorted the refugee group to a camp that Mustafa claims was run by a political outfit. He reassured them they could rest before leaving on buses for Damascus. Their precious ID cards were in his possession but he demanded nothing. Mustafa says reverently, "He took no money from us. He treated us well and did us a favor. We saw him for thirty minutes and we will remember him all our life."

It was not this man's fault that the refugees were unable to travel to Damascus as he had promised. Bomb attacks in the capital meant transport there was stalled. Mustafa grimaces when he remembers the consequences of this stoppage: "They gave us mats to sleep in the open air. There were stray dogs all around us." After two weeks, Mustafa decided to proceed to the city of Hama instead. They passed more checkpoints along the way and "were counted like sheep to make sure no one escaped," but their ID cards were restored to them once they reached Hama. Mustafa smiles: "They told us we were now free to go and to do whatever we wanted in this land!" But Mustafa and Asma were determined not to hang around for long. After being screened as safe to travel within their own country, they left for Lebanon as fast as they could, settling in Beirut to try to bring their traumatized family back on its feet again.

8

WELCOME TO LIBYA

"GOD SAVED ME"

"**W**hen you see the corpses in the desert, it's shocking. I was totally nauseated. I saw many dead of hunger, of thirst. I thought I'd end up like that. But I couldn't stop or turn back. I was there. What could I do?" Amadou is trying to make me understand what his clandestine journey through North Africa and the Mediterranean Sea was like. He assures me, "There are many who have experienced more than I have. But I can only talk for myself, and if I don't explain well, you won't understand. It is good to understand that the journey is very dangerous and that many died. I thought I was finished but God saved me. He said, 'You come here alive.'"

"Here" is Marseille, in southern France, where I am introduced to Amadou in a beautiful church in the heart of the city. A group of volunteers teaches French to refugees and migrants in the parish house. Amadou comes for his class and, later, consents to be interviewed. Not that I need to ask many questions. Amadou is a natural storyteller. Memories flow as he tells how he left Guinea, his homeland in West Africa, and made his way toward Europe along one of the riskiest routes in the world, known as the Central Mediterranean route. Until recently, this route was the most popular among refugees leaving from sub-Saharan Africa and North Africa.

"The Sahara Desert, Libya, the sea: everything was so very difficult! Ah! I will never forget those times. I don't even know how to explain and, when I try, it plays with my mind." Amadou repeats himself to stress the horror of it and gets worked up because he cannot do justice to what he lived and saw. Equally lost for words, Omar displays his scars instead. Omar sold two cows to get the money to travel from his home country of Mali and ended up in the Sicilian town of Catania. He traveled the same route as Amadou. He says, "The desert was very difficult and risky. Anyone who passed there will understand." He laughs a bit, as if at the absurdity of stating the obvious. "Let me show you; I have something here." Rolling up his shirtsleeve, Omar reveals an ugly scar on his upper arm. "This was done with a gun. It was the smugglers in the desert. They asked for money. If you don't have anyone who can send it to you, then you are in trouble. I said I have no money and no family, so they shot me." The bullet in his arm persuaded Omar to call a Malian friend of his who worked in Libya to wire the ransom money.

Smugglers and traffickers control the Central Mediterranean route, just as they do all of the clandestine pathways that most refugees are forced to use. Refugees have no option except to resort to these routes, because even if they have a passport, they are rarely granted visas to travel legally. For the profiteers who manage their fate, refugees are merely cargo that passes through several hands, bought and sold each time. Every time, however, it is the refugees who must redeem the price placed on their life. Throughout their journey, they are given barely enough to survive and squeezed for all they can give.

Miguel is a teenager from Cameroon who went first to Nigeria and then onto Niger, where he met an Algerian man named Abdul Aziz, whom he describes as "a bit like a *capo*." Miguel uses the Italian word for "boss" because he is in Sicily now. Miguel says meeting Abdul Aziz was a mistake and it soon becomes clear why. First, Abdul Aziz took Miguel and his friends to work with him on a farm in Algeria, and then he announced that they were going to work for his friend. A Libyan man came and took them to Libya. Miguel says, "We didn't know what they concluded among themselves, but we had no choice. When we came to Tripoli, this man made us prisoners and forced us to work. Abdul Aziz had sold us to this man."

Refugees tend to describe Libya with fear and loathing. Miguel refers to the country as "Hell. Everything is bad there. Everyone has a gun and everyone uses it how they want. Down there, even if you are a human being, it doesn't matter. If you are black, your life is not important." Years after the fall of the dictator Muammar Qaddafi, Libya remains deeply divided and unstable. Rule of law eludes the fragmented state, where an internationally recognized but weak government in Tripoli is challenged by a parallel structure in the east. The country is awash with militias and terrorist groups vying for control. In April 2019, the volatile situation took a nosedive. Military strongman Khalifa Haftar, whose forces support the parallel government in the east, launched an offensive on Tripoli. The fierce clashes around the capital had refugees in greater danger than ever. Many were trapped in detention centers close to the fighting. On 3 July 2019, at least fifty-three refugees, including six children, were killed after air strikes hit Tripoli's Tajoura detention center in which hundreds were being held. Shelling inside residential neighborhoods also displaced and killed Libyan civilians.

Even when Libya is relatively calm, refugees are very vulnerable because arresting or kidnapping them is a lucrative game. They could be whisked off the bus, apprehended in the street, or rounded up at home. A Somali man once told me, years ago, how he and his friends always slept in their shoes in Tripoli so that they could get up and run if someone came knocking on their door at night. Smugglers and militias regularly imprison refugees for ransom in centers described by the UN as "forced labor camps" and "makeshift prisons." Libya's weak law enforcement agencies not only do nothing to stop the problem, but also arbitrarily arrest refugees and detain them. The conditions in all the detention centers, official and otherwise, are typically inhuman.

CRUEL EXTORTION

Miguel ended up in a prison run by a smuggler, who forced him to become a slave to redeem the price paid to Abdul Aziz for him. The teenager soon experienced another common tactic to extort money: "In this prison, they used to beat us and call our family from our phone, and even record everything on video, so our relatives could listen and see, and send money. They got black people like us to beat us. I was attacked with the tip of a rifle; I still have the scars on my arms—look!"

Amadou was also thrown into an unofficial prison run by smugglers. He could not stand the cruelty of the guards. "The worst thing in prison was when they came to beat us every morning so we would call our parents. Who could I call?" Amadou had only his elderly mother back home and she was in no position to send him money. Actually, he was longing to call his mother because he had not talked to her for months, but he could not even dream of doing such a thing then. Instead, Amadou tormented himself with thoughts like, "What if she could see me now?"

Amadou told the prison guards he had no family. "So they beat me. Oh! No! No! No!" He shakes his head and exclaims vigorously. "They beat you everywhere with tools like this." He points to the telephone cable wire and heating pipes running along the walls of the room. "If your relatives say, 'Today I will make the money transfer at 10:00 a.m.,' and 10:00 a.m. passes and they have not made the transfer . . . ah! No! No! No! The guards come and beat you, how they beat you." Amadou becomes more and more distressed as he goes back to those terrifying moments. He points to the middle of one of his palms. "They got a *drill* and they drilled a man's hand in front of my eyes. They pierced it. They forced him to dial the number of his relatives and they showed them. This made me cry, I tell you. I was so afraid."

These horrors are perpetrated in suffocating spaces that are over-crowded, dark, and stiflingly hot. Amadou describes the prison as so crammed that "you cannot even lie down to sleep." Then there was the hunger. "If you eat in the morning, you wait until the next morning to eat again. They give you half a piece of bread," he says, indicating how small, "and you must eat that. For how many months can a man survive on that? It's impossible. Sometimes I spent entire days without eating, without drinking." Miguel tells a similar story, saying they were treated like beasts, but then corrects himself: "Not even beasts are treated like that. People died every day. We were all in one room, a tightly shut room without ventilation. It was so hot, we couldn't even breathe. You ask for water and they give if they feel like. No one talked. We were not even allowed to cough."

Forbidden from opening his mouth, Miguel found consolation in prayer: "You cannot talk to the people around you but you can talk to God in your heart. I knew I would survive, if it was his will, because he alone holds your fate in his hands." Miguel has a speech impediment that makes it difficult for him to articulate some words. Nonetheless, he does his best to describe what he went through. He draws, thinks furiously to search for the right words, and is endlessly patient when I do not understand. Like Amadou, he attributes his survival to divine intervention: "I am here because the good God wants me to be here. I could have died." Miguel becomes emotional when he remembers Libya, not least because "when I tell people here, they don't believe."

The UN, human rights NGOs, and journalists bear out the testimony of Miguel and Amadou. The situation has been like this for years, even in Qaddafi's time, and shows no signs of changing. In fact, it has been getting worse. Thousands of refugees are held at any given time in at least thirty detention centers known to exist across Libya, official and otherwise. Outsiders have been allowed into only a handful of the official ones. By all accounts, whipping, rape, and other abuses are common, as are disease outbreaks. There is a great scarcity of food and water. Some people are there for months.

Some do not leave alive. "Every week, someone dies. The guards take them out and throw their bodies in the desert," says Amadou. This is what happened to him—only Amadou wasn't quite dead yet. Rather, he collapsed out of sheer terror, at the thought of what would happen to him when his deadline to find the ransom money ran out. "They told me, 'If you don't get the money, we'll break your arms or drill your hands.' A week before my turn, God helped me. I fell ill. I was so sick, I couldn't even walk. I thought I was going to die; everyone thought so. They threw me in the desert and left me for dead because they thought I'd never leave the center on my feet."

GOOD SAMARITANS

After being thrown out of prison, Amadou had another stroke of luck. A Good Samaritan found him lying in the desert in an emaciated and wounded state. "An elderly man was passing with his herd of livestock and found me there. He welcomed me to his house and took me to hospital. He did everything for me," Amadou recalls gratefully. The Good Samaritan was a Libyan named Abdallah. He looked after Amadou for months and would have been happy to host him for longer. But Amadou wanted to leave Libya at any cost and pleaded with his benefactor to help him: "I asked him to have pity on me, that my desire was to cross the sea." After attempting in vain to persuade Amadou not to go to Europe, Abdallah found a smuggler and paid for his guest's trip to Italy himself.

Amadou headed for the coast. En route, robbers attacked the group he was traveling with. "My money was sewn into the lining of my trousers; they took it all. They took everything, even my phone, and I lost all my contacts, including Abdallah's. At least we managed to run away from them." Amadou reached Tripoli penniless. He missed *mon vieux* ("my old man"), as he fondly referred to Abdallah, and was disappointed by what he describes as the selfishness of fellow Africans: "I spent three days without eating, only drinking. You see people sitting in front of you. They eat; they give you nothing. Eh, the Africans! Yes, yes, my 'friends.' They do not have the spirit to share with you."

The family of Emil also found a Good Samaritan in Libya. God knows they needed one. The family fled together from Guinea because the mother was ordained by custom to take her own mother's place as the village circumciser, to carry out the traditional practice known as female genital mutilation (FGM). Emil's mother did not want to take on this preordained role, but refusal meant incurring communal wrath, so she left with her family.

Upon reaching Libya, the family faced the usual litany of abuses. Emil was sixteen years old at the time. Imprisoned twice and forced to work, he was hit on the head with a rifle for having the temerity to ask for payment. What is especially shocking about the plight of Emil's family is that Libyan prison guards did not even spare his two tiny brothers, ages one and two years, respectively.

Whoever arrested them came to the place where the family was staying in Tripoli. Emil calls them "bandits," but he uses this term for all those who kidnapped or attacked his family in Libya. Emil was spared that time because he happened to be on the roof, getting some sun. Once he realized what was going on, he stayed put. Emil's father and two younger brothers were taken to prison. The guards beat his father badly and turned on the little boys, too, hitting them on their testicles. As usual, the abusers wanted money, and Emil's mother was at her wits' end.

And then their Good Samaritan appeared in the guise of a Libyan man called Mahomet who visited the family at home and learned that three were in prison. "He helped us; he had my father and brothers freed," says Emil. Who Mahomet was and why he paid the ransom,

Emil does not know. All he can say is that Mahomet turned up "by the grace of God." The family saw no more of him. Shortly afterward, their landlord evicted them because they could not afford to pay the rent. But they did hear that Mahomet had gone to ask after their welfare again.

Eventually, Emil's family managed to arrange for their trip across the Mediterranean, and they moved to sheds close to the shoreline that housed refugees waiting for their first opportunity to leave for Europe. After a month, their turn arrived. Emil describes the scene: "The women went on the boat first, so my mother went with my sister and the baby. My father, my two-year-old brother, and me, we waited our turn. They led us, ten by ten, to go on the boat." When their turn came, there was a sudden commotion on the beach and the rattle of gunfire. The "bandits" had come to disrupt the smuggling operation. Things happened in seconds. The boat immediately took off and those left behind scattered in panic. Emil says he saw people fall, dead or wounded. In the chaos, he lost his father and brother and ran away.

After lying low for some days, Emil cautiously made his way back to the shoreline and stayed there alone, day after day. He believed he was the only one of his family to have survived and did not know what to do. Then a smuggler who arranged the departure of the boats asked Emil, "Why are you always here? The others leave but you stay back. It's as if you don't know what to do." Emil poured out his story and the man promised to help him. True to his word, he managed to get Emil a place on a departing boat and "God willed that I arrive in Italy." Emil was alone in the world, or so he thought at the time, but at last he felt safe.

9

"SAVING LIVES IS NOT A CRIME"

"THEY JUST GOT TOO TIRED"

Amadou made his way to Europe eventually. After he had made arrangements to travel, the days of waiting sorely tried his spirits. All the episodes of his life that had led to this nerve-wracking point flashed before his eyes, filling him with sadness and regret. He says, "I lived the worst moment of my story before we crossed. I asked myself, 'Why did this all happen? Why did I have to leave my country?' I actually cried because it was so difficult for me."

Amadou left Libya in a nine-meter (thirty-foot) zodiac crammed with some 150 people. He dreaded the journey and was justified in doing so. The stretch of Mediterranean Sea between Libya and Tunisia at one end and Malta and Italy on the other has become one of the deadliest in the world. More than 14,500 deaths have been recorded along this route since 2014. There are many reasons why it is so risky, among them that smugglers use increasingly unsafe boats, fill them to overflowing, and send them out even in bad weather. In 2017 alone, nearly three thousand travelers were reported missing. Although the number of deaths decreased in 2018, the *rate* actually increased when compared to the number of people who arrived safely on Europe's shores. These grim statistics are only the tip of the iceberg: who knows in reality how many people died anonymously and are lost forever in what has become a mass graveyard?

Thirty-six of Amadou's fellow travelers died during the three-day voyage. He guesses it was because they were very weak for some reason or other—because of pregnancy or because their hands had been pierced in prison, for example. "They just got too tired," he says. The bodies of those who died were thrown overboard. Amadou finally reached Europe when the boat touched the shores of Lampedusa, a tiny island that forms part of Italy.

Abdoulaye, a man from Mali who now lives as a refugee in Rome, made the crossing twice, reaching Sicily the second time. The first time, the dinghy sank, and a quarter of those on board died. The dinghy measured approximately six by two meters (twenty by six feet) and had 120 passengers. When Abdoulaye saw how many people were piling into the boat, he demurred. "The smugglers told me, 'You have two choices: you go or we shoot you,'" he says. This was Christmas Eve of 2014. The sea was very rough and the dinghy sank after an hour. "I could do nothing except save myself. Luckily, I could swim. It was so sad to hear people screaming for help," Abdoulaye says. "Some started to swim but didn't make it. They gave up after about an hour because they were too tired." Abdoulaye and the other survivors swam back to Libyan shores. "At first, I was afraid, but then at a certain point I stopped being afraid, because I had nothing left to lose."

The sea crossing is so risky, and the odds of dying are so high, that we might be tempted to shake our heads in disbelief at those refugees who make the choice to try anyhow. Perhaps we fail to grasp the pure meaning of "nothing to lose" and to realize that actually there is no choice. An Eritrean refugee named Abdel Mohammed elaborates on this beautifully: "It seems to me that the boats are not a means of transport but a destination in themselves. People run to reach the boats. They don't care if they sink, or if they arrive in Italy or Tunisia or wherever. They don't care; they just want to get away." The desperation so intensely described by Abdel does not make the dangers of the journey any less terrifying. But it does propel people to embark—knowing they may never reach the other side—because they do not see any other way out.

Abdel is a deeply reflective man who has spent most of his life either on the move or reflecting on the experience. The first home Abdel knew was a refugee camp in Sudan. His family lived there until he was nine years old. One morning, he poked his head out of their tent and found that all the other refugees had left to go back home to Eritrea because its thirty-year liberation war with Ethiopia had ended. "We were in the middle of nowhere. I found no children to play with. It was such a big shock for me. I had lost everything I knew," he says. Abdel's family returned home to Eritrea too. Less than ten years later, Abdel left to escape conscription. Unlike other Eritreans I met, Abdel came from what he calls a "totally militarized family." He says, "My father, brother, sister, nephew all joined. There was not one who did not take up arms. In my father's house, you'd find weapons more than food."

Abdel made his way to Libya, found a job, and spent some years there. Then the civil war that would oust Qaddafi broke out in 2011. "When the war began, it was unreal," he muses. "You didn't know where reality started and ended." What Abdel knew was that his days in Libya were numbered. Both sides in the war targeted sub-Saharan Africans: anti-Qaddafi forces accused them of being mercenaries in the dictator's pay, while Qaddafi himself decided to send migrants to Europe in droves to punish the international military coalition that was backing the rebels fighting against him.

Abdel says, "I knew Qaddafi was letting us go only to blackmail Europe. But Tripoli was a city where everyone was armed, even children. It was a place where you could die like a dog and no one would know or ask after you." A reluctant pawn in Qaddafi's hands, he knew there was no other way: "It was too bad to get into a boat knowing you are only a tool and knowing you cannot go back because there is war. In the end, the only destination was that boat."

For Abdel, nothing in his life took as long as the few steps from the shore to the boat: "When I walked from the beach to the boat, it's incredible, *that* was the longest journey I ever made. Walking in the water, I saw people throwing off their clothes and anything that would slow them down. I saw people walking naked to reach the boats." Abdel confesses to getting goosebumps when he thinks about it, even now. "The moment I got in that boat, I was so happy. I cannot imagine ever being as happy again as I was at that time. I couldn't care less where I was going; I just wanted to get out of there."

Abdel has harsh words for those who condemn the decisions made by refugees: "Many stupid people want to put themselves in the shoes of a mother who put her children in a boat. They say, 'How could a mother do that?' But did you see what the mother saw and lived through? Do you know?"

To this day, Abdel is afraid of Libya. He realized the extent of this instinctive fear when he participated in NGO search and rescue missions at sea, departing from Catania, where he lives now. Once, he spent the night on a rescue ship and woke up to find a message on his phone welcoming him to Libya because the phone had automatically picked up a Libyan network. "It was a surreal moment for me," he says. "For a minute, I thought, 'What's going on?' How could I forget I was on the ship and that I was there for a mission? I forgot everything when I saw those words 'Welcome to Libya.' I was scared."

For Abdel, the moral of the story is this: "Just try to imagine the people who live there to this day. They wake up every morning to find themselves there, they go to the water to leave, and they are stopped. This is something that really disturbs me."

SEEING THE REALITY

The European Union (EU) has no problem blocking refugees coming from Libya despite the meticulously documented exploitation and torture they suffer there, and the terror invoked by mere mention of the country's name. In a bid to stem arrivals to European ports by sea, the bloc has been funding, training, and equipping the Libyan coast guard to intercept smugglers' boats and take them back to Libya, where the refugees face detention in appalling conditions. It is unthinkable, inhuman, but it happens. Those sent back are men, women, and children who have the right, under international law, to seek asylum from persecution and who must reach a place where they can realistically claim and find it. Libya does not qualify as such a place.

For much of 2018 and 2019, Italy, the landing point in Europe of most refugees who travel by boat from Libya, adopted a hard-line approach. The right-wing government refused to save refugees in distress at sea and closed its waters to NGO rescue vessels that did so. It also criminalized their lifesaving efforts. In just one example of official bullying, in 2019 Italian authorities ordered the seizure of an NGO rescue ship, the *Mare Jonio*, and accused it of aiding illegal immigration because it defied the government's order not to bring the refugees on board to Italy. Although the island of Malta, the other EU border state in the Central Mediterranean, allowed some NGO rescue vessels to disembark, it also intimidated and prevented them from doing their altruistic work. All this is tragic news for those attempting the sea crossing. In the first half of 2017, NGOs performed 40 percent of rescues in the Central Mediterranean.

In mid-2018, the German captain of an NGO rescue vessel called the *Lifeline* found himself facing charges in a Maltese court. After saving more than two hundred refugees in distress at sea, Claus-Peter Reisch adamantly resisted pressure from the Italian and Maltese governments to hand them over to the Libyan coast guard. The saga continued for a week, until Malta reluctantly accepted the refugees. The country then proceeded to charge Claus-Peter with steering the *Lifeline* into its territorial waters without the necessary registration and license.

"The Libyan coast guard wanted us to hand over our guests to them and I denied this," said Claus-Peter. He was in Malta to attend one of his court sittings when I caught up with him at the hotel where he was staying. Claus-Peter was staunch in his straightforward belief that "to save lives is not a crime. It is a human duty." He was quite sanguine about the charges leveled against him because he was sure that any magistrate in his senses would see he had done nothing wrong. More to the point, the case was trivial compared to what really mattered: "We are just talking about a blue sheet of paper. In four rescue missions, we've saved more than 450 people from drowning. With this in mind, I can stand upright in the court."

Nearly a year after he was charged, the court found Claus-Peter guilty of steering the *Lifeline* into Maltese waters without the required registration and fined him ten thousand euros. He is appealing the verdict, which Mission Lifeline dismissed as "disastrous." Claus-Peter does not have the slightest doubt he did the right thing, both morally and legally, despite accusations to the contrary. He answers to a higher court, if you like.

For Claus-Peter, allowing his passengers to be taken back to Libya would have violated international law. There was no way he was going to tamely hand them over to the Libyans. He told me, "We had people on board who were pushed back three times, and what they reported was so awful, because the torture started again when they were sent back." The *Lifeline* doctors warned him that a Somali man on board might die within hours if he did not receive medical care, because he had been tortured so badly in a Libyan prison.

Claus-Peter recalled how the Libyan coast guard radioed the *Lifeline* shortly after the crew rescued 234 refugees from two dinghies. "The coast guard wanted to come alongside us in the high seas, which is very dangerous," he said. Claus-Peter allowed two officers to board the *Lifeline* unarmed. The news petrified his passengers. "You could see the fear in their faces, like this was the beginning of the end. They became very quiet," he remembered. "We told them to be calm. 'Don't worry,' we said. 'Don't show you are afraid. We'll do everything for you.'" One young man from Bangladesh dropped to his knees, crying and shaking, and clung to Claus-Peter's legs. He begged, "Please don't give me back. Before I go back, I will jump into the sea." Tears came to the captain's eyes, too, at that moment. "I promised him I would never do that."

Claus-Peter was as good as his word. The captain of the Libyan coast guard laid claim to the refugees, saying, "It is my waters. It is my people," to which Claus-Peter replied, "These are free people, not yours." After the Libyans left, the tension on board abated, but Claus-Peter had seen and sensed enough fear to convince him not to relent. "When I came back from my discussion with the Libyan coast guard, the man from Bangladesh fell on my neck, and I could not breathe because he pressed me so strongly. He was crying. I said to myself, 'If an adult man is doing this, maybe you could imagine what happened to him in Libya.' I will never forget him in my life."

Claus-Peter started thinking about getting involved in search and rescue missions in 2015, when record numbers of refugees flooded into Europe, especially via Greece. Traveling from Sardinia to Greece on his sailing boat, Claus-Peter saw dinghies packed with people and the flotsam of children's toys and shoes in the sea, and he wondered how he could help. He took the plunge because "I wanted to see the reality for myself" amid raging debate about what Europe should do with the refugees who were arriving: "Should we save them, push them back, let them into the EU?" he summarized. On his first mission in 2017, Claus-Peter saw the reality and decided to do search and rescue again. When I asked him to describe what he saw, he replied, "Dead bodies floating in the sea; the wounds of those tortured; people with trauma, with open eyes that look into nothing, empty eyes."

The moment that stayed with Claus-Peter most of all was a surprisingly tranquil one. The *Lifeline* was stranded at sea, and mothers with babies and little children were sleeping in the ship's hospital. "It looked so peaceful," he said. "There was a girl of maybe three years with a soft toy, from us, and she had it in her arms." His eyes misted over as he spoke: "There are some pictures that politicians need to see with their own eyes and not talk about things they have never seen in their lives. It is without respect."

It is strange that Claus-Peter was on trial for doing the right thing. It is bizarre that he should need to state the obvious to supposedly civilized governments: that life comes first and that he could not in good conscience return people to be tortured, raped, and killed. But this is nothing more than a frightening sign of the times, when governments unscrupulously wield the letter of the law to crush its noble spirit, and get away with it. While they attempt to bully NGO rescue vessels into submission, people are drowning or being dragged back to Libya.

Claus-Peter sought "reality" in a bid to make sense of Europe's politicized debate around illegal immigration, and he found it in the people whose lives are at stake, in their eyes, their faces, and their stories. Due to the *Lifeline* saga, Claus-Peter found himself in the media spotlight in Germany and did all the interviews he could, up to seven a day, to raise awareness about what he discovered in the Mediterranean. He did so reluctantly but knew it was a responsibility he could not shy away from, because the costs might be too great, and not only for refugees.

Claus-Peter was clear that his aim was not only "to do something for refugees" but also "to stop the far right." Across Europe, far-right parties have made depressingly impressive electoral gains in recent years, and the overall tone of political and media debate is dominated by their strident anti-immigrant rhetoric. Claus-Peter added, "I think it is in everyone's interests to stop this far-right current because, around eighty years ago, we had the same thing and everyone knows where it ended."

10

ALWAYS LOOKING FOR A BETTER PLACE

FREE AT LAST

Tigiste left Eritrea by force after being declared a fugitive in bizarre circumstances. The guard who had sneaked her out of prison to be his sex slave was intent on covering up what he had done. To get rid of Tigiste, he dispatched her to the border with Sudan, where she was handed over to a Sudanese smuggler who took her to the capital, Khartoum. Installing her in his home, the smuggler raped and prostituted Tigiste. This time, she managed to escape within weeks.

Although Tigiste was free at last, she cut a forlorn figure all by herself. She sat helplessly in the street and cried until an Ethiopian woman approached her and asked her what was wrong. Tigiste calls her "my angel" because she gave the broken girl a job at her restaurant, a place to live, and the chance to piece her life together again. But there was more suffering in store for Tigiste. "I found out I was pregnant. I did an abortion because I didn't know who is the father," she says. This is something that torments Tigiste to this day: "That's why, still, I can't sleep. Every night, everything comes in my mind."

Despite all she had been through, Tigiste did manage to get on with life in Sudan. She worked in her friend's restaurant and took a correspondence course in accounting. But Tigiste never really felt safe. For one thing, the smuggler wanted her back. Policemen turned out to be tormenters, too, going to Tigiste's place, threatening to send her back to Eritrea, and sexually abusing her. They would leave her in peace only once they had extorted money from her. When an Ethiopian friend suggested that she leave for Libya, following in the footsteps of countless refugees, Tigiste took to the idea. To me, she offers an explanation for deciding to move again: "In my life, I've always wanted to find a better place, and this is why I continued my journey."

Tigiste skims over the details of her journey to Libya through the Sahara. Once in Libya, she found well-paid work relatively quickly, keeping house and doing the accounts for a man who ran a business in the city of Benghazi. Things were looking up on the personal front too: Tigiste embarked on a relationship with an Ethiopian man and got pregnant, which was good news for her this time. Her boyfriend left her shortly afterward, but Tigiste was looking forward to being a mother. She lived together with other Eritreans and Ethiopians in containers that served as their communal homes.

And then ISIS turned up, taking advantage of the civil conflict in Libya to carve out a space for itself. ISIS made its mark by beheading and shooting dozens of Ethiopian and Eritrean Christians and releasing videos of the killings. Their grisly communications sent a chill around the world. Tigiste and her friends stayed indoors, but ISIS came after them. Once, some twenty masked men banged on the door of their container home and yelled for everyone to get out. All were lined up and shot dead. Tigiste says, "I saw with my eyes people dying just like this, all my friends, Eritreans, because they were Christians. The ISIS man threatened to hit me if I cried." Crying now, as she relives the moment, Tigiste clenches a fist and brings it close to my face to demonstrate.

Tigiste believes she was spared because she was pregnant. But worse was to come. ISIS fighters slit the throat of another friend, so that his blood sprayed all over Tigiste. Another time, they set a man on fire. Tigiste shudders: "I can still smell the odor of burned flesh." Ever since she witnessed them, these ghastly images keep company with Tigiste. When she tries to sleep, the final moments of her slaughtered friends fly back. "If I close my eyes, I see their faces. I see my friend, and how it hurt when they cut his throat," she says between her tears. "I still hurt when I think of these things. I can't forget because I see too many people dying. I can never forget in my entire life. That's why I have too much headache. I can't sleep. I feel bad because they were my best, best friends."

JOURNEY TO EUROPE

After her son, Ermias, was born, Tigiste knew her days in Libya were over. She decided to move again, this time to Europe. "The big problem was that I could not take my baby on the boat, so I decided to leave him with my friend, because she was legal." Tigiste's friend was an Ethiopian woman named Mrs. Getachew. She planned to return to Ethiopia, which she could do safely because her papers were in order, and the two women decided that she should take Ermias with her. For Tigiste, the way ahead was heartbreaking but clear: "I had two choices: I die with my baby in water or I save him. If I die, he has someone who loves him, because she has no children and she is a good woman. I believed her."

Tigiste's first two attempts to leave Libya by sea were doomed to failure. The first time, most of her fellow passengers drowned. "We were in a wooden boat and we met a storm leaving the Libyan coast. Only a dozen or so survivors returned to Libya out of two hundred who left. The sea took all the others," she remembers. The second time, the smugglers told one of the refugees to drive the boat, but he had no idea what he was doing and the passengers urged him to return to port when the sea started to get rough.

The third time, a week later, they prepared to set off again, in a dinghy this time. About two hundred people wanted to board and the waves were already picking up. To balance the boat, the smuggler picked out people at random and had them thrown into the water. He turned to Tigiste, pointed to her backpack, and asked, "Shall I put you in the water or will you put your bag in?" Tigiste had all her documents, including the contact number for Mrs. Getachew, carefully wrapped in plastic. But she knew it was useless to plead and instantly replied, "Put my bag in the water, please." Today, Tigiste mimics the smuggler's callous selection, pointing with her finger: "You and you, out." She adds bitterly, "He did not even ask; he just did it. They don't care about you. They don't care if you die. They don't know you. Why should they care about you? They just want their money."

Tigiste was ordered to sit in the middle of the boat "because I am light." She says this saved her because many of those who were seated on the edge fell into the water and drowned, some pushed in by the people near them. "In the middle, we were sitting in water mixed with petrol that burned our skin. But at least we survived." This was in February, and the freezing water soaked through the seven layers of clothing that Tigiste had put on in a futile attempt to keep warm.

The boat landed safely in Sicily. Tigiste kept moving and managed to cross, undetected, from Italy into France by train. Without a fixed destination in mind, she disembarked in the city of Marseille, a few hours from the Italian border, because she was sick and tired of traveling. In what must have been a familiar feeling by now, Tigiste was alone in a strange place. She slept in the train station for five days and then in the street. The only thing Tigiste knew was that she felt completely drained: "I was so tired, because since I was six, I have been traveling. Whether this was my destiny or not, I don't know, but I needed to rest here and so I slept in the street."

11

FORTRESS EUROPE

NORTH AFRICAN SPAIN

Melilla is a beautiful anachronism, a city on the northern Moroccan coast that forms part of Europe. Spain won Melilla and Ceuta, a sister enclave farther up the coast, through military conquest nearly five hundred years ago and refuses to give them up. Today, the historic neighborhood of Melilla houses medieval barracks and fortifications that for centuries have stood firm against crashing waves and invaders. A strong military presence still pervades the city, and one of its claims to fame is the last statue of General Francisco Franco on public display in Spain; all those on the mainland have been removed. The modest statue lurks under the city's massive fortification walls, a reminder that the former dictator rose to prominence in Melilla, as a young officer of the Spanish Legion. Another claim to fame is that Melilla was the first town to revolt against the Popular Front government in 1936, precipitating the Spanish Civil War.

There is an air of surrealism in North African Spain. Melilla's pristine wide avenues pack in plenty of architectural influences: elegant art nouveau balconies overlook sinuous mosaic benches, reminiscent of Gaudí, that bask in the shadow of bulky, propagandistic fascist monuments. The parks are beautifully kept, the beaches likewise. The Spanish population of Melilla includes many citizens of Moroccan birth or descent. The city is open to Moroccans, who can come every day to work or to visit, using their identification documents to do so, while many others live there in what might be called an irregular situation. Catholic, Muslim, Jewish, and Hindu communities exist side by side. And then there is the invisible presence of unwelcome guests who have gate-crashed the city: the new "invaders" that Europe is so busy building bastions to keep out.

As the only territories where the EU shares a border with Africa, Melilla and Ceuta have inevitably become magnets for refugees. This is where you see what Fortress Europe looks like in practice. The border between Melilla and Morocco is ringed by a triple row of high fences with curls of barbed wire and a ditch on the Moroccan side. On both sides, border guards man the fences. The Moroccan guards are criticized for their brutality in dealing with those who try to cross irregularly. The Spanish stand accused of pushing people back without bothering to find out whether they need protection. Despite the formidable obstacles, 6,800 refugees got into Ceuta and Melilla in 2018, mostly to Melilla. They came largely from Africa and the Middle East.

Sometimes Melilla and Ceuta hit the news, especially when hundreds of people rush the fences at once and try to clamber over. By and large, however, the daily struggle of refugees to get into these two cities unfolds far from the public eye. Their repeated efforts to scale the fences or to slip through the border-crossing points reveal the depths of their determination. A Palestinian man from Gaza tells me he tried to cross ten times and, each time, Moroccan border guards thrashed him. He succeeded the eleventh time. Another Palestinian, Hassan, says, "The Moroccan guards showed no respect for anyone, young or old." Hassan is in his late fifties. When he attempted to cross the border with his fifteen-year-old son, only the boy managed. When Hassan finally reached Melilla himself, he spent months battling red tape to get his son back, despite having all of his identification papers.

Syrians, Palestinians, and Algerians stand a fair chance of blending with the crowds at the border checkpoints because they conceivably can pass for Moroccans. Sometimes they get a passport for several hundred dollars. Still, slipping through the checkpoints is always touch and go, with windows of opportunity that might last only seconds. Families can easily get separated. After we meet Hassan, my translator tells me about a six-year-old Syrian girl she met recently, in the course of her humanitarian work. The girl was left behind in Morocco after her parents and siblings managed to cross. When the girl was reunited with her family in

Melilla a month later, she was caked in dirt and lashed out at anyone who tried to go near her, much less touch her.

On the other side of the border, in the Moroccan town of Beni Anzar in the province of Nador, I meet a gracious Congolese woman and her teenage daughter at a shelter located within the compound of the Catholic Parish of James the Apostle. The woman's leg is encased in plaster up to the knee; she broke it while trying to climb the fence. The Diocesan Delegation for Migration runs the shelter and a clinic thanks to sisters and priests from different congregations. Migrants frequently turn up with injuries sustained in their futile attempts to reach Melilla.

A priest based there recalls a fifteen-year-old boy who had managed to jump the fence but lacerated his arms with razor wire in the process. As soon as he set foot in Spanish territory, he was promptly pushed back to Morocco, where border guards thrashed him. The boy spent hours walking to the hospital in Nador, and from there he was referred to the church clinic. The doctor said it would take several hours to stitch his wounds because they were so many and so deep. What moved the priest most of all was the boy's resolve: "He explained to me quietly that he was now convinced that *je dois faire la mer* ('I must go by sea'). No beating would sway his simple conviction."

Once refugees set foot in Melilla, their only wish is to be transferred to mainland Spain as soon as possible. During their stay, most are warehoused on the edge of the city, out of sight and out of mind, in an overcrowded center called CETI (Centro de Estancia Temporal de Inmigrantes). When I visit CETI, distressed young men accost us on the way out, looking for answers. "I am here for three months. Why no *La Salida*?" asks one. *La Salida* ("the exit" in Spanish) is the weekly ferry that goes to mainland Spain and is eagerly awaited. Another says angrily, "They see refugees, not human beings."

ANOTHER DEADLY OPTION

The option to enter Spain by land is not the only one open to refugees. There is another: to travel on inflatable rubber dinghies or wooden boats to the mainland, usually to the southern region of Andalusia closest to Morocco and Algeria. Spain's maritime rescue service, Salvamento Marítimo, intercepts some of the boats and brings them to shore. In the second half of 2018, Spain became the top entry point to Europe with 65,400 arrivals, as the Central Mediterranean route became less traveled. Many factors led to the decline of this route, including Libyan coast guard patrols, the refusal of Italy to allow refugees to disembark, and the dangers of the route, especially in Libya. However, the Western Mediterranean route to Spain is also pretty deadly. As the number of crossings rose, the number of deaths at sea on this route quadrupled over the previous year.

When we arrive at the church clinic in Nador, the sisters have just taken in survivors of a boat that sank. Two women and a child drowned. Boats are taking off even when the sea is rough because of a crackdown by Moroccan police attributed to a new installment of EU funds for their "border management." The refugees live in makeshift camps in woodland around the town while waiting for their chance to cross the border. Police have stepped up their raids on these camps, destroying whatever they find and putting the refugees on buses, to be dispatched to the other end of Morocco or the border with Algeria. Many beg their way back to the Spanish border.

Unfortunately, in this part of the Mediterranean, the EU is also seeking to distance refugees from its own territory. The strategy with Morocco echoes that adopted with Libya and consists of pouring money into national coffers for "border management." The problem with this blueprint is that the EU is entrusting the protection of people in need to countries that have proved they cannot shoulder the responsibility. As for the Spanish government, it has joined the race to the bottom: in 2019, it banned NGO rescue vessels from departing from its shores and was accused of dismantling the rescue operation of Salvamento Marítimo, which has saved thousands of lives.

12

LOOKING FOR LIFE

"I WANT TO SEE MY FAMILY AGAIN"

Habib knew nothing about Melilla until he reached Nador. After escaping from his captors, who had enslaved him for fifteen years, Habib gradually made his way north to reach the coast facing Spain. It was a smuggler who told him there was a way to enter Europe on foot and that there was no need to go by sea. He eventually managed to enter Melilla by rushing the crossing point with a group. The guards caught some, but Habib was one of those who got away.

In Melilla, Habib is eager to make a life for himself but insists that he badly wants to find his family, too, something he would have to retrace his footsteps to do. Although this might sound like mission impossible, to track down relatives in the vast desert after all these years, Habib is resolute: "I want to find my parents; it's all I desire. I don't know if I am Algerian, Moroccan, or Mauritanian, but I remember a family life, and I want to find this family I left when I was ten years."

Habib's eyes glisten when he brings up vague memories of his family. "I remember an older sister who got married—there was a party, and I was the youngest. I don't know if I have other brothers and sisters. I remember my mother; she had a tattoo on her forehead and plenty of hair framing her face, because she was young. My father was young too." Habib's parents won't be young any longer if he ever gets to meet them again. But he refuses to lose hope. "I can look for them because they are nomads, and there are precise places where they have paths, and I'll go to search for them there. I will ask people of the region."

Habib has another quest: "Not only do I want to see my family again, I want to find all the people who helped me on the way, to thank them." He says there were many: "Since I escaped, I always found people to give me food and shelter, to open the doors of their home to me." The first night after he ran away, Habib stayed in a mosque in Ramlia. Later, he would approach men as they left the mosque after prayers, or boys who were roughly his age in the street. He explains, "They were not afraid of me because we talked the same language, and so they took me as their family, as one of them. I shared my story with them. You must tell them or they will not trust." Habib remembers staying for ten days with one family because it was Ramadan, and he could not travel in the intense heat while fasting. His new friends introduced him to others. "They'd come shopping to the next village I went, ask me if I was OK, and try to help me go farther, asking the people of the place to help me too."

There was only one time during his journey that Habib was frightened: when he found himself in the underbelly of Fez, Morocco's second-largest city and cultural capital. Habib headed to the bus station to travel north and was surrounded by people who lived on the streets. "Fez was different," he says darkly. "It was very bad. There were so many thieves. Even if you have nothing, they steal the nothing you have. I'm alone too. I lived on the street, so I understand those who are homeless and try to help them when I can. But in Fez, I was afraid because even the children were violent and desperate; they took drugs."

After fifteen days, Habib scraped together enough money for bus fare by doing odd jobs. He went to Nador, and on to Melilla, where he now lives in CETI and has bonded with friends who are like him. He says, "I have met many others from the Sahara who lived my life, and we have made a family together. When one has a shower, the others watch his things, so no one will steal them and like that."

"ALL I WANT IS TO WORK AND HAVE A PEACEFUL LIFE"

Daoud is one of those friends. Daoud made it to Melilla thanks to the unexpected generosity of a total stranger whom he approached to ask for drugs. This was in the bus station of the Moroccan city of Agadir. Instead of complying with his request, the stranger put Daoud on a bus to Nador. Before this chance encounter, Daoud had traveled a long way in a lonely bid to find a life better than the slavery he had known so far.

Once he had escaped his captors in the Algerian desert, he hitch-hiked his way to the heavily fortified border with Morocco. His heart sank when he got there. Both Algeria and Morocco have built high fences along their border, each accusing the other of allowing smugglers and terrorists to cross. Algeria also has added a deep trench and a berm. The only way to get across was to pay a smuggler, but Daoud had nothing. He spent a month at the border, begging for food, until a fuel smuggler gave him a tip: why didn't he try to sneak through when fuel was taken across the border at night?

When Daoud followed this advice, he found a bustling operation under way. As he describes it, smugglers were busy taking fuel from one side of the border to the other, which they did by creating bridges of big bales of straw in the trench. The bales were brought every night by trucks, deposited, and later collected. The smugglers bribed border guards and were allowed to operate as long as they removed all signs of their illicit operations by dawn.

Watching and waiting, Daoud was approached by a man who asked him why he was sitting there in the cold. Daoud told his story and, to the inevitable demand for money, replied that he had none. What happened next takes some imagining: the man was the driver of an excavator used for the smuggling operation. Moving quickly and furtively, he told Daoud to climb into its clawlike bucket. Then he set the machine in motion and deposited Daoud on the other side of the border. "I was so afraid to get in. I didn't know if he was going to throw me out or put me down," says Daoud. "The ditch was so deep and there was barbed wire all along the border. But he deposited me on the other side and I was in Morocco."

Daoud had crossed relatively close to a holiday destination. As he walked, he met tourists who gave him food, and "one man gave me his own clothes and shoes." Daoud decided to trust the police with his story but found himself in prison as a result, accused of being a smuggler because he had no identification papers. He spent six months inside. In proof of either how miserable he was before or how well he was treated in prison, Daoud did not want to leave. Bizarrely, when the police came to release him as abruptly as they had imprisoned him, he asked if he could stay. But they threw him out, so he resumed his journey.

Daoud crisscrossed Morocco, heading first to Marrakesh and then to Agadir, walking for days to get there. He went to a bus stand, hoping to find a place to sleep. Like Habib, Daoud was immersed in a crowd of homeless people. It was there that he decided he wanted to try hashish or sniffing glue or silicone, which were all for sale. But when Daoud approached a man to ask him for any of these substances, he was in for a surprise. The man asked him why he wanted to try drugs. Upon hearing Daoud's story, the man bought him a bus ticket to Nador and gave the driver money to give to Daoud only if and when he reached Nador. Daoud is grateful to the man who slipped in and out of his life and unexpectedly did him a good turn: "He was a good person, to live that life, and to remain good."

And so Daoud found himself in Beni Anzar in Nador, a place he had not even known existed until the day before. As soon as he landed, homeless people swarmed around him again. He remembers with a grimace, "They touched me all over to see if I had anything they could take." He lost the shoes the tourist had given him: "Since my shoes were newish, they took them and gave me older ones."

Crossing into Melilla from Nador proved to be relatively easy. After being caught and beaten once, Daoud got through the checkpoint. He has already been in Melilla for a year when I meet him, living in CETI. Staying at the mammoth center is a sore trial for residents, who complain about the overcrowding, clashes, and constant theft, and who stay only because the alternative is living on the street. And yet Daoud does not grumble, either about CETI or about the months he spent homeless in Melilla until he managed to get into the center.

Quite the contrary: Daoud is grateful. "Here people help you even if you can't explain. You just open your mouth, and they help you. The police also give us food," he says. "When I lived on the street, the police knew we were not troublemakers. I am peaceful; all I want is to work and to have a peaceful life." Despite the privations of his life in Melilla and the delay in his transfer to mainland Spain, Daoud seems happy. "In all my life, the only year I feel I have lived is this year in Melilla," he says. He has just one problem: "I'm programmed to wake up at three or four every morning and to work, because I've been working since I opened my eyes to this world. The only thing that stresses me now is that I can't work."

I can't help feeling hope and fear at the same time about Daoud's prospects in Europe. Will he find the happiness that has eluded him so far? He asks for so little, and my fear is that even that will be denied him, because of the limited and unimaginative policies that dictate who is deserving of protection.

"FORCED TO FOLLOW THIS RHYTHM"

For Adil, getting into Melilla was not complicated at all. When he received the police summons to go for interrogation because of his intense involvement in the Hirak movement, Adil knew he had to leave Morocco immediately. Moving fast, he went to the Spanish enclave, which his beloved Rif region surrounds. He presented his passport, walked serenely through the border, and checked into a hotel. Adil says, "That night, I slept soundly and securely for the first time in months, because I was not afraid of being arrested." The next morning, he made a formal request for asylum. "They tried to find out if I was really involved in the demonstrations or just making things up to get my papers," he recalls. "Then they saw I was saying the truth, and that I had lived the situation, so it went well."

The impact of his new identity hit Adil as soon as he went to CETI and saw where he was supposed to live: a tent he describes as over-crowded, dirty, and smelly. He says, "I could not believe it. This was never my plan. I felt my life had been turned upside down. I had become a refugee." Sleeping in the tent, Adil developed severe back pain and was taken to a hospital, where he was introduced to a Spanish family that offered him a place to stay. Adil was relieved but kept fretting so much that his entire body was immobilized by a kind of paralysis that lasted for weeks. He puts it down to stress because "I was thinking so hard."

Adil was discharged after a month in the hospital and gradually got used to Melilla. But this is a lonely life in limbo for the young man. He wants more than anything to go to the Netherlands, where he says there are many Moroccans from the Rif who could help him find his place there. However, a year after submitting his asylum application, Adil has not yet received a reply. And he has not been called to take the weekly ferry to mainland Spain. This is a long wait by any estimate. In Melilla, a city Moroccans can enter so easily, Adil lives in fear: "This place doesn't help me. I can't sleep well. I'm afraid. It's not safe because anyone can come and stab me."

Adil is at pains to explain that he became a refugee because he was forced to do so and not because he had any desire to go to Europe. He insists, "I am forced to follow this rhythm now. It was not my choice."

13

"I TRUST MYSELF"

QUEST FOR THE ESSENTIALS OF LIFE

"I trust myself." This is Jospin's motto. If indomitable will, natural ability, and perseverance were an assured recipe for success, then Jospin would have realized his dreams several times over by now. The teenager could easily have qualified for a slot in one of the famous self-improvement books of Dale Carnegie. But so far Jospin's dreams have eluded him because, much as he may trust himself, success is not up to only him. His fate is also ruled by luck and by the forbidding immigration policies that govern access to better-off and safer parts of the world than the one in which he was born.

Jospin left his native Cameroon when he was sixteen years old to find what he calls "a normal life." Abandoned by his mother when he was only a child, Jospin was entrusted to the care of an elderly woman who sometimes left him without anything to eat for days. "I worked hard every holiday to pay for my school fees and food," he says somberly. "She would give food for one day and then leave for a whole week."

Meanwhile, growing social unrest was having a direct impact on Jospin's life. Jospin belongs to Cameroon's Anglophone minority, which makes up one-fifth of the country's population. Street rallies and strikes by the minority to protest against their marginalization led to a standoff with the government. Security forces cracked down violently on the protesters. Jospin describes the situation matter-of-factly as a "struggle between the people and the government. They didn't recognize our rights and we were calling for our rights."

Jospin recounts how the situation deteriorated: "The army stopped school; no one was going, and police were beating people in the street, even shooting sometimes." Once, Jospin was arrested, briefly imprisoned, and roughed up. "Police saw three or four of us going to school and they arrested us because they accused us of forming a group. They kept us at the police station for three days and beat us every morning. Then they let us go and threatened to imprison us if they ever saw us again." Jospin decided that enough was enough.

His quest for the essentials of life, which so many of us take for granted, took Jospin on a walking and cycling trek across six African countries. He wound up in Melilla, where he is stranded. Jospin is making the most of the impasse he has found himself in, as I discover at Geum Dodou, a day center for refugees and migrants in Melilla run by women from two Catholic congregations. Jospin feels at home here, in a room crowded with young men and boys who drop in to pass the time. Most sit in a row in front of computer screens, headphones clamped over their ears, either watching a movie or listening to music. Others are charging their phones or calling friends and family. Small groups chat together. The atmosphere is relaxed and friendly.

Jospin and I find a desk in a corner, and he leaps into his story without further ado, oblivious to the background noise. He keeps his head down, the short dreadlocks that frame his cheekbones falling over his face. Speaking in a level voice, Jospin starts from the beginning, when his intention was to go only as far as neighboring Chad and to study there. But once he arrived, attacks by Nigerian terrorist outfit Boko Haram and the general air of insecurity ("Everyone had a gun," he says) soon put paid to that idea. Jospin was disappointed because "I went to be protected, not to be killed." His brief sojourn in Chad taught Jospin a lesson: "If people know you are a stranger, they can treat you as they like."

Jospin doubled back to Cameroon before heading to Nigeria and, from there, to Niger. Since he had no money, Jospin sought work at every opportunity, to get himself to the next leg of his journey. He knew he was being exploited every time, working hard for a pittance or for nothing, and had no choice but to put up with it. Whenever he could, this remarkable young man simply set off on foot, walking hundreds of kilometers from one town or village to the next.

Winding his way through Niger, Jospin got a reality check when he inquired about traveling to Libya. He wanted to take the bus and was asked, "Passport? No? Then you are a migrant." As a migrant without any documentation, Jospin understood that the only means of transport open to him were clandestine, risky, and expensive. He says succinctly, "If you don't have papers, you must travel *ilegalmente*."

So, instead of going to the bus station, Jospin was directed to a house where he discovered many others waiting to travel to Libya. He paid for his trip and was locked in the house until it was time to cross the Sahara Desert. He traveled in a vehicle with some thirty passengers from Nigeria, Guinea, and Cameroon. "We sat like this in the car," says Jospin, crouching forward and hugging his legs tightly to his chest. "The person in front of you sits on your legs. In the desert, you have nothing to say. The driver can do what he wants."

ESCAPE FROM LIBYA

After three days, the stiff travelers reached the town of Gatron, typically the first stop in Libya. "Then everything changed," says Jospin. "They locked us in a house and threatened to shoot us if we tried to leave. If you had no money to pay for food, you were not going to eat." Jospin's time in Libya is an echo of the usual catalogue of kidnapping, abuse, and forced labor. I find it hard to follow how many times he changed hands and how many times he was accused of not paying his way and made to fork out money again. It is difficult to get a word in edgewise to ask for clarification, because Jospin is speeding through his story at a relentless pace, intent on telling it from beginning to end. He is so absorbed in the task, it is almost as if he is talking to himself.

One detail particularly sticks out in his story: a fellow Cameroonian "rescued" Jospin from one prison only to put him in a prison he ran himself. This was in the town of Sabha. Jospin was desperate because he was being beaten daily to get his family to send money but had no one he could call. Then the Cameroonian turned up: "He told me he had bought me and saved me because I was his brother." Jospin still had to buy his freedom from his compatriot but was reassured he was getting a special reduced rate. Then his Cameroonian captor decided to pass Jospin onto another "brother" of his. Jospin had to agree, because "where could I run to in Libya? You are not safe; they will get you a second time."

Jospin was allowed out only to go to work to redeem the debt imposed on him. He says, "It was very difficult. After you finish your day's work very well, they point a Kalashnikov at you and tell you to run. They do not pay me, so how can I pay?" He remembers how once he was robbed as well as exploited. "They took three of us to the Sahara to do one job. They got big sticks and starting beating us to give them all the money we had. We could say nothing." Jospin eventually managed to escape and made it to the border with Algeria, where he could not afford to pay a smuggler to take him across. Jospin was afraid his captors would catch up with him if he stayed in Libya to earn more. "This is business," he says. "They all knew each other, and they would find me."

Jospin decided to take yet another risk: "I said, 'Whatever, I will cross on foot.' I just took my bag and started walking." After a few kilometers, a Libyan driver gave Jospin a lift for his "small" money and told him to make up the rest if they met again someday. During Jospin's hikes over thousands of kilometers, some drivers did offer him a ride, but they usually wanted something in return. Jospin's conclusion: "They can't help you for nothing." One driver picked Jospin up when he was about to collapse but dropped him off soon afterward because "he told me to do something very bad, if I want to continue with him, and I said I cannot."

On the Algerian side of the border, Jospin worked to save enough for a bus ticket to the nearest town, five hundred kilometers (311 miles) away. But then he faced the same reaction as before: no passport, no ticket. The price of traveling *ilegalmente* was more than twice his savings. Anxious to put as much distance as possible between Libya and himself, Jospin again resolved to walk. "I trust myself. I said, 'Five hundred kilometers is nothing.' I took water and much bread and put it in my bag. I said, 'I'll drink my water small-small.' And I went slow-slow at night. After two days of walking and sleeping, bread and water, I was going to die."

FROM ALGERIA TO MOROCCO

When he reached the next town, Jospin faced a familiar predicament: he needed money to continue his journey. The problem was that he was not alone in looking for work. He was traveling along a well-worn route of refugees from central and western Africa to Morocco and onward to Spain. He is matter-of-fact about this: "Everyone is traveling. We didn't come here to stay. Everyone says no job. They don't trust us because they know we can leave today or tomorrow." After days of searching, Jospin found a job in a restaurant kitchen and saved a tidy sum, enough to buy a bicycle and have some change to tide him over until the next stop on his itinerary.

After cycling in the sun for more than one hundred kilometers (sixty-two miles), "I was a dead man." When a car stopped to offer him a lift, it was all Jospin could do to drag himself in. The driver offered to take him the rest of the way on one condition. Whatever the condition was, Jospin was not prepared to accept it, because he hastily made up an excuse and jumped out of the car. The next driver to stop offered Jospin a lift as well as a job: to guard a house under construction at their destination.

The deal sounded too good to be true but Jospin accepted anyway. Installed at the construction site, he helped the workmen: "I worked all the time they wanted." But he soon realized "it was the same story: if I kept working, I was losing." Jospin eventually got half of what he was owed, sold his bicycle to raise more money, and set off again. He says, "I left the very night I asked for my money again. I trust myself. I always take to my legs. I walked and walked for fifty kilometers [thirty-one miles] and then one car helped me."

In the ancient city of Oran, his last stop in Algeria before the Moroccan border, Jospin decided that he was going to have to trust someone other than himself. He knew that going to the border alone would be too risky, because he had grasped something of the unwritten "law" that governs the clandestine route, a law dictated by smugglers and "bosses" from the migrants' countries of origin. He explains, "If you arrive alone, they take you to a place like a prison of your community, and wait until you pay money for your travel." Still, Jospin was reluctant: "You don't know whom you should trust." He settled on a boy from Ghana because the boy had contacts in the smuggling networks. With his new friend,

Jospin went to a "bush house" run by a boss from Ghana and paid the fee demanded to stay in the house and to be taken across the border.

It goes without saying that Jospin and his friend crossed the border *ilegalmente* and without any idea of where to go. They went as part of a group of thirty men. On the Moroccan side, the guards arrested and punished them severely. "They beat us all night and asked where our guide was," recalls Jospin. "No one talked and they sent us back across the border." The guards warned them, "If we catch you a second time, we break your legs and kill you." Five heeded this warning, as "they had been beaten too badly the night before." The rest, including Jospin, succeeded in getting into Morocco the second time around.

The next stop was another house and another boss. The house was locked and the boss demanded more money from Jospin, who surrendered the last of his savings and named his destination: "I want to leave to *la frontera*" ("the border" in Spanish). Jospin was taken to Nador by car. He knew nothing about the border or his likelihood of crossing it. He just knew he wanted to get there.

MELILLA!

In Nador, police arrested Jospin almost immediately, when he went to look for a bus. With a single-minded intent that ignored caution, Jospin dared to ask where "the fence" was—that is, the barrier between Nador and Melilla. "I was ready to take any risk. I said, 'Where is the fence? We did not steal anything. Why do you arrest us?'" Jospin escaped from the police station by jumping over a back wall. All he cared about was getting to the fence. After feverishly running around in circles, Jospin found someone to tell him that he needed to head for the town of Beni Anzar, where the border crossing was.

In Beni Anzar, Jospin discovered that the refugees lived in makeshift camps in woodland around the town. They stayed in groups, each one with a chief. "I was told I had to pay the boss for my right to stay there. This boss was from Mali. I had nothing, so they said I have to leave if I don't pay." Jospin returned to the town, slept on the street, and begged in the market to get the money to buy his place in the camp. A weary five months followed. Every day, Jospin crept to the market to rummage in dustbins for discarded vegetables. He explains why: "Each group cooks for itself; you cannot eat alone. I had no money, so I had to look for food to say to the chief, 'This is my contribution.'" Every night, Jospin tried to cross the border with the others. Every time, "the police caught us, beat us, and let us go."

In the end, Jospin admits, "I was tired." His fatigue is starting to show in the interview too. His spirits sag as the end draws near. He tells how, after repeatedly and unsuccessfully trying to enter Melilla with a group, growing frustration spurred him to try to enter the city alone. Spanish police caught him scaling a wall at the shore, where the fences ended. Jospin was using hooks to get a better grip for climbing. Still with the hooks tied to his hands and feet, he raced through the streets of Melilla but failed to shake off his pursuers. In a last-ditch attempt, he ran to the beach and waded into the sea. "I knew it was finished," he says ruefully. "I stayed in the water for more than an hour. One of the police swam towards me. I moved backwards until I was up to my mouth in water." The next thing he knew, Jospin was in a hospital bed. He discovered that the police had also approached him from behind, in a boat, and knocked him unconscious.

Jospin was arraigned in court and accused of aggression against the police, because of the hooks, although he did not threaten the police with them. He is aggrieved about the summary proceedings: "I had no time to explain. They just tell you what you did. All that my lawyer told me was that I had committed a crime. He didn't ask me what happened." Pushed by his state-assigned lawyer to accept culpability to avoid a trial, Jospin "was forced to say yes—I had no choice," and was given a suspended sentence. The judge converted the sentence to an expulsion order, which was not executed because Jospin applied for asylum. More than a year later, Jospin still has received no reply to his application, and the threat of deportation to Cameroon in case of a negative decision looms over his head. Melilla is an open prison for him.

This knowledge is a bitter pill to swallow: "After all I did to get here, I cannot leave. I have nothing else to do." He is genuinely puzzled about his sentencing ("How they judge me, I don't know"), and a sense of injustice rankles: "My problem is what happened with the police. Everything they say is false but impossible to restart." Jospin has a new lawyer now, from an NGO, but the outcome remains uncertain. So near and yet so far, Jospin tries to be stoic. "It's not right but it's no problem.

Maybe one day I'll leave Melilla but I don't know when. Now I am just waiting."

"A BETTER LIFE IS WAITING OUT THERE"

Jospin was not always so sanguine about his fate. When he came to Melilla, the shock of his sentence hit him hard. "I hated this place when I arrived," he admits. Jospin withdrew into himself. Although he went to the day center for language classes, he sat alone, the hood of his sweater hiding his face. The sisters remember how Jospin would be the first to leave once class was over. Then one sister tried to pull him out of the despair he had sunk into and made a critical discovery: running was Jospin's life.

This was twenty days before the 2018 edition of La Carrera Africana, one of the biggest annual events in Melilla, a fifty-kilometer (thirty-one-mile) ultramarathon through the city organized by the Spanish Foreign Legion, which is garrisoned there. People rallied round: Jospin got a coach and running gear in record time, and the sisters prepared lunch for him every day so his diet would be spot-on. Then there was a setback. Jospin suffered a leg injury and was strongly advised not to run. He ran anyway. Jospin's lawyer, Diego, describes the end: "It was a very cool moment because Jospin came into the race already injured and we were almost sure he wouldn't reach the finish line. When he arrived, a lot of people from CETI and we were waiting for him. We cheered, the speaker announced Jospin was arriving, and he was in the newspaper the next day."

When the Africana comes into the conversation, Jospin promptly recovers his good humor, which had dissipated when he relived the dismal end to his journey. "The Africana was the best moment I passed here," he beams. "They don't know what it represented for me." I guess it signaled the rebirth of hope for Jospin, without which he is nothing. Now Jospin trains every day, taking Diego with him if he turns up on time. Jospin returned to the Africana in 2019 and finished twelfth out of more than 1,500 participants, clocking in at one hour and forty-three seconds. He has taken part in more races in Melilla, winning several medals. "Running is here and here," Jospin says, tapping his head and his heart.

Running has kept Jospin going in more ways than one. Today, he is well known in the city and attends the local secondary school. He has come a long way from the boy who sat huddled in a corner of the day center; now he teaches Spanish there to fellow refugees. In one class, Jospin wrote on the flipchart, "Don't cry . . . there is a better life waiting for you out there in the future." This message of hope epitomizes Jospin. Except for the time when he nearly buckled under the blow of getting a criminal record, Jospin resolutely refuses to give way to despair. He keeps talking himself into a more positive frame of mind, not so much denying the obstacles as refusing to let them dictate his pace. He says, "I am not tired; I have to do something more. I am not afraid; I know that when I leave this town, I'll do something better. I trust myself. I know all is not lost."

14

THE GAME

BEWARE OF THE DOGS

Rafi is a serious boy, unsmiling, with a hint of defiance in his eyes. This is how he appears at an aid center for refugees in Belgrade. Rafi and his dad have just come in from the freezing cold. The only time that Rafi smiles, dispelling the gravity that sits ill with his ten years, is when his father talks to, hugs, or kisses him, which he does frequently. Rafi is the son of Farid, who left Afghanistan after Taliban threats materialized in the abduction and killing of his three cousins. Farid and Rafi traveled through Pakistan, Iran, Turkey, Greece, and Bulgaria to reach Serbia.

Serbia is not their destination—it is just another stop on the way— and for weeks they have been trying to cross another border, so far without success. This is the clandestine route to Europe mostly used by Afghans. Like all other illegal pathways, it makes for a highly risky and tough journey, one organized by smugglers. Refugees go through a gauntlet of steep mountain passes, river crossings in overcrowded dinghies, and abuse from border guards. Despite the risks, some nine thousand Afghans arrived in Europe via Greece in 2018.

Farid's journey was especially difficult because he had to look after his son. He remembers with gratitude the help of fellow travelers who took turns carrying Rafi and who made sure that father and son always had enough food. At times, however, Farid and his companions were helpless to protect the boy. The worst moment came in Bulgaria, when the police set dogs on them at night. Rafi was so terrified that he screamed and screamed until the skin of his lips became mottled, or so it seemed to his father. When Farid tried to fend the dogs off, one bit through his jeans and skin—he rolls up his trouser leg to reveal the scar. In terms of most frightening experiences, Farid actually puts the dog attack on a par with the killing of his cousins by the Taliban. Sometimes, the horrors and humiliations that people face on the road to seek asylum are as bad, if not worse, than what they escape.

"The Bulgarian police took everything we had," says Farid. "I had some money saved for when my son got hungry, and they took it. They took our food, water, clothes, and mobile. They emptied our backpacks and cut through the straps. Then they gave us the torn bags in our hands and pushed us back across the border to Turkey."

Virtually every refugee I meet who has passed through Bulgaria remembers the experience with fear. Hussein, the university student who escaped Taliban wrath after he foiled a bomb attack, left all his belongings behind in Turkey to make sure Bulgarian police did not get their hands on them. Word was that they set fire to everything they confiscated. Hussein does not even have a photo of his mother in Belgrade because he left his mobile behind. To call her, he must borrow a phone from one of his friends.

Hakeem, whose father disappeared in Afghanistan, describes Bulgaria as the worst part of his trip. "Police forced us to lie on the ground for four hours while their dogs ran over us. One of my friends was bitten," he recalls. "Then they took us to a closed center. When they wanted to move us somewhere else, we asked if we could go to get our stuff from our rooms. They hit us and refused to listen. I had to leave everything behind."

Another young Afghan man I meet in Belgrade was pushed back from Bulgaria twice, after being beaten not only with batons, but also with branches that the border police cut from the trees. "When we tried to escape, they released the dogs," he says. Each time, he was sent back to Turkey without his shoes, because policemen took them. Still, he might consider himself fortunate compared to Jafar, also from Afghanistan, who says he was stripped naked three times, twice in Bulgaria and once in Greece, before being pushed back to Turkey. Jafar eventually entered Europe on his sixth try.

HIDE-AND-SEEK

The centers I visit in Belgrade are both run by local Serb NGOs. One brings back memories of the day center in Melilla: young men clumped in groups charge their phones and sit in front of computer screens. Both cities are transit zones. In Melilla, there are young men from sub-Saharan or North Africa, while in Belgrade, the vast majority are Afghan men and boys. When I visit Belgrade in December, they flock to the centers to shelter from subzero temperatures outside, since many of them sleep rough or squat in empty buildings. All are there with one purpose in mind: to "go for the game."

The game: this is what refugees call their tortuous attempts to cross borders covertly. Sometimes it takes dozens of attempts to get from one side to the other. When I meet Zahid, who left Afghanistan because he refused to become a Taliban spy, he has just come back from the game. He had managed to get quite far, going through Croatia to reach Slovenia—just. Zahid explains dolefully how police scanners at the border discovered him stowed away in a truck. "We said we wanted to ask for asylum and could we stay in Slovenia?" Zahid splays out the fingers of both hands and continues with a smile: "We offered to leave all our fingerprints and even toe prints if necessary." Zahid was pushed back to the Serbian border and dumped there in the snow. His predictable conclusion: "We will try again as soon as we can, no other choice."

Leaving their fingerprints in the wrong country is a big worry for those who want to seek asylum once they reach the EU. Most have a very clear idea where they want to end up, usually Germany or France, or wherever they have relatives and an established community of their own to welcome them. However, a controversial and cumbersome EU law, called the Dublin Regulation, threatens their plans. This law obliges people who are caught crossing the EU external borders irregularly to file their asylum claim in the first country they reach. Their fingerprints are put on a Europe-wide database and used to trace their journey to its beginning in the EU. Asylum seekers and EU border states alike resent the Dublin Regulation. Asylum seekers, forewarned by smugglers and those who have gone before them, assiduously try to avoid being fingerprinted before they reach a country acceptable to them. Luck plays a big part. Jafar mentions friends of his who arrived in Serbia just a few days ago, left again immediately as stowaways in trucks, and managed to reach Germany undetected. "And I have been here for three months," Jafar says.

Those caught in this bizarre game of hide-and-seek do not expect to get off lightly. Jafar says philosophically, "I was beaten in all the games I tried." Although Bulgarian police might be among the worst offenders in the game along the Balkan route, they are far from the only ones. Abuse at the borders appears to be motivated by the desire to punish and to deter refugees from making future attempts to cross. As a deterrent, the strategy fails signally because people will keep trying, dozens of times if they have to, and resign themselves to being abused every time. It is hard to tell whether such abuse is officially sanctioned (if unstated) policy or unchecked sadism on the part of border guards, or a mixture of both. It is fair to say that not all the members of border forces engage in abuse, even in places where it is rife.

Many refugees cross the Evros River, which runs through the Balkans, to get from Turkey to Greece. Another young man, whom I identify as "Tiger" in my notes because he is fidgeting with a small plastic tiger he finds on the table, tried the river route. Tiger remembers being beaten and stripped naked by Greek border guards who looked like boxers. Croatian border guards are also feared for their brutality. Tiger was in Bosnia when the lifeless body of a Pakistani man was brought back from Croatia. "They said the Croatian police beat him and he died soon afterwards," Tiger recalls. "At the hospital in Bihac, they were showing his photo around and asking if anyone knew who he was, to identify him." He continues with a mirthless laugh, "If you are trying to go to Europe illegally, this kind of thing can happen."

Given the welcome he received from Croatian police, Tiger is not surprised that another met his death at their hands. He says, "When we tried to cross from Bosnia, they pushed us back to the river, until we were in water up to the chest. About fifteen police started hitting us, not looking or caring where the blows went—eyes, mouth, nose, head, chest—just blindly kicking and hitting." And yet, when we meet in Belgrade, Tiger immediately warns me that he does not have much time because he is going for the game again that very evening.

Farid and Rafi have already tried to cross into Croatia twice. "They beat me but not Rafi and took our mobile and money," says Farid. "If you try to run, they beat you more." Hakeem agrees that those who try to escape are more severely punished. He uses his hands to approximate the size of the heavy black batons they used to bash him and the others. "If you try to escape, they will beat you badly, and they don't care where they hit. When they call you to stop, you must freeze," Hakeem insists. "You can't move, not even to pick up your bag or to close your jacket; you don't have the right." Hakeem tried to hide his phone. The guards found it and broke the USB port with a screwdriver so he would no longer be able to charge it. He got his broken phone back, but one guard snatched it again, threw it on the floor, and ground it to pieces with the heel of his boot.

Ali, an eighteen-year-old amiable giant from Pakistan, avers that Croatian forces "beat you like a donkey." He keeps saying this over and again. The punitive element emerges clearly: "They brought us back to a camp near the border. Then they called us, one by one, and two of them beat each one of us with police sticks like a donkey. It is, like, to punish you. When it was my turn, I shouted out loud, 'My turn!'" Ali escaped with bruises. One of his friends fared worse: the guards broke his leg. Ali says, "I put him across my shoulders and we walked back to Bihac, in Bosnia, where we took him to hospital."

Until they can move on from Serbia, life remains in limbo for refugees. Most live outside official reception centers because they are unhappy about the conditions inside and because it is more difficult to make arrangements to go for the game from there. Ali has been living outdoors, in a Belgrade park, for three months now. He has made some friends from Afghanistan and they live together in a tent they made of stones, wood, and plastic sheeting for the roof. "We spend our time like brothers. When they are with me, I don't feel alone. It is very good for me," he says. Ali cannot afford to buy a sleeping bag or even a blanket to ward off the bitter cold. He covers himself in a big jacket and an extra pair of trousers. He laughs: "At night we never sleep. We are like commandoes."

Ali survives thanks to money sent by his mother via Western Union from Pakistan. His mother and sisters are all he has; he is an only son and his father is dead. Ali is in constant communication with his mother. During the interview, he calls her with his webcam, so that he can introduce us to one another. Ali cannot bring himself to tell his mother that he is sleeping outside. "She would be so worried if she knew," he says. He must lie to her, which he hates doing, and tell her that her beloved son is doing just fine and has nearly reached his destination.

15

CRISIS OF COMPASSION

A FIFTY-FIFTY CHANCE

Whatever the route, the game is a gamble played against heavy odds and with punishing losses, and yet refugees feel they have no option but to play. They are well aware of the odds; more than one has put them at fifty-fifty in conversation with me. They have seen death or felt it at very close quarters along the way. Zahid had a lucky escape when crossing the Evros River to go from Turkey to Greece: "Our dinghy sank when we were in the middle. I grew up near a river back home, so I can swim, and I helped others to reach the shore too. But it was scary and so cold." Zahid first pulled to safety three men who were floundering near him, and then he jumped back in the water to rescue two more. Everyone survived.

Refugees dread those passages of the journey they know to be especially hazardous. Just as they fear Bulgaria, many will tell you that Iranian border guards have orders to shoot those crossing irregularly. Ali remembers the thoughts flitting through his mind when he went from Iran to Turkey in a group of hundreds of silent travelers in the dead of night. "If I die here," he worried, "my mum and my sisters won't know anything about me. They don't know where I am and I couldn't tell them because I'd be dead." Iranian guards did not catch him or his companions.

Others were not so lucky. After Hussein crossed from Iran to Turkey, he spent days in Istanbul waiting anxiously for a friend, Hamid, who was supposed to follow a day or so later. But Hamid never turned up. Hussein recalls, "I waited and waited. Finally, I called his brother in Afghanistan and asked where Hamid was, what happened to him. His brother said Hamid was dead, shot with a bullet to his neck at the Turkish-Iranian border. The smuggler told them all to run fast and the border guards fired. His body was sent home to Afghanistan." The news shocked and saddened Hussein: "Hamid was my friend; we were together in Tehran. He was twenty-five, so young, so young. He left Afghanistan because he had to. He was innocent, and he was killed. Hamid was unlucky."

The whimsical intervention of fate plays a critical role in every game, for better or worse. But in this game, the stakes are too high to entrust to luck, because the lives and limbs of the players are on the line. What's more, the two sides are unevenly matched: exploited desperation on one side and officially sanctioned pushbacks and abuses on the other. And yet the game is played thousands of times every day at borders around the world, because an estimated fifty-fifty chance of survival is always better than what the refugees left back home.

Zahid is unequivocal about this: "The Taliban was worse. Here, we are tired, hungry, thirsty, but nothing compares to the Taliban." Farid agrees wholeheartedly: "I feel safer and happier here, even sleeping outside in the freezing weather, rather than staying in Afghanistan. If I think this is tough, on the other side I remember my family waiting for me there."

What is the family of Farid waiting for? The answer is found in his "biggest wish," which is to reach his destination, France, and to bring his wife and children to join him. This plan, which might be closer to wishful thinking than real possibility, is a very common one. Most of the refugees going for the game at Europe's borders are men traveling alone. There is more than one reason for this, depending on the situation. Young men have fled Syria in droves to escape forced recruitment by the army. The same applies to Eritreans. However, many men undertake the dangerous clandestine journey alone in the hope that they will find a safe place where they can bring their family to join them. That their plan is often foiled by restrictive immigration policies does not diminish the selflessness of their decision. They miss their loved ones terribly, and sometimes it is years before they see them again (if ever), either back where they started or, if they are very lucky, together in their new home.

OPEN-DOOR POLICY

Just a few years ago, the clandestine route from Turkey to Europe via Greece looked and felt very different. In mid-2015, Germany declared an open-door policy to welcome people escaping the war in Syria. In that year alone, 1.3 million refugees came to Europe from Syria and many other countries, especially Iraq and Afghanistan. In just one day in October, ten thousand people crossed the Aegean Sea from Turkey to Greece.

Entire families traveled together, parents with their children, elderly and disabled people, some in wheelchairs, barely able to move. Most borders along the Balkan route were open, and people rushed from one to the next, intent only on reaching their destination, which was overwhelmingly Germany. In German and Austrian train stations, volunteers and well-wishers greeted refugees with applause, candy, hot drinks, and signs of welcome. In Croatia, NGOs at transit points welcomed the travelers with hot drinks, clothes and shoes, blankets and backpacks.

The moment did not last long. Within weeks, panicked European governments were scrambling to stem the flow of refugees. By early 2016, countries along the Balkan route had shut their borders, leaving thousands of refugees stranded in abysmal conditions in Greece, one of the EU countries least able to look after them due to its own debt-ridden crisis. In another sign that compassion was drying up, support surged for a populist party in Germany's regional elections. In March 2016, the EU signed a shameful readmission deal with Turkey, and that was that.

Under this confused deal, anyone arriving illegally on Greek shores and found to be ineligible for asylum would be returned to Turkey. For every Syrian refugee returned from the Greek islands, another would be resettled from Turkey to the EU. Nothing of the sort has transpired. Instead, the deal traps refugees on the islands, forbidding them from moving to the mainland until their asylum claim is processed. Packed to overflowing, the islands host refugees in extremely poor conditions, many in tents and containers.

Nonetheless, the EU now refers to 2015 as a crisis that is mercifully over, done and dusted. It is quite true that the number of refugees reaching Europe has dwindled since then. By the end of 2016, arrivals were not even one-third what they had been the previous year. The number dropped further in 2018, to around 144,000, a mere one-tenth of arrivals at the height of the "crisis." However, the complacent stance of the EU begs a global perspective. UN statistics reveal that the world's poorest countries give asylum to more refugees than the EU does. Developing regions host 85 percent of the global refugee population. Germany is the only European representative in the top-ten list of countries that host refugees.

The crisis the EU is suffering from is arguably a crisis of compassion. Meanwhile, around the world, unabated catastrophes continue to uproot more than forty-four thousand people every day. Take the countries fled by most people seeking asylum in Europe in 2015: four years later, the war in Syria dragged on, Afghanistan still suffered the deadliest fighting in the world, and Iraq remained monumentally unstable and violent. But for the EU, out of sight means out of mind, and this is why it has pumped so much money into shoring up its external borders and paying Libya, Morocco, Turkey, and other countries to look after refugees, increasingly tying compliance to other benefits.

A RAW DEAL FOR AFGHANS

Hakeem tells me wistfully, "I wish one day the borders will be opened like they were in 2015. When the border is open, I'll go to France." His wish is likely to remain unfulfilled. However, even in that brief time of golden opportunity, Hakeem would have stood a good chance of being rejected because he is Afghan. From what I saw and heard when I moved along the Balkan route in early 2016, the authorities were dangerously confused about Afghanistan. Afghans would be allowed through the borders one day only to be turned away the next.

Most EU countries remain reluctant to protect Afghans, who make up one of the largest groups of asylum seekers in the bloc. More than four hundred thousand Afghans applied for asylum in the EU between

2014 and 2016, and more keep coming, although evidence reveals that they get a raw deal: their applications are pushed to the end of the queue, there is a huge backlog in processing them, and they get a high rate of rejections. Ultimately, less than half of those who apply get protection. Back in 2016, at a huge shelter in the German city of Munich that housed some 850 people, I met an Afghan man who was furious about the delay in processing his application. "I've been here for nine months and I don't even have an interview date. At least hear me out—I have proof; my body itself is proof." The man was full of scars. Back in Kabul, five masked men stabbed him fifteen times, accusing him of not being Muslim enough, of working for Americans, and of other "crimes."

Afghans suffered a backlash when Europe's spontaneous spurt of compassion in 2015 dried up as quickly as it had appeared and policymakers moved to reverse the onward flow of movement. In late 2016, the EU signed an agreement with Afghanistan to facilitate returns, once again showing its propensity to link compliance with delivery of aid. Immediately afterward, Germany chartered its first deportation flight to Kabul, and more than ten thousand Afghans were sent back within months. Those who are not deported, following the rejection of their asylum application, remain in Germany on "toleration," as their shaky legal status is known. This just means they have not been deported—yet. They do not get the benefits that come with officially bestowed protection and can be kicked out anytime. This is a common plight across Europe, and one experienced not only by Afghans: the *sans-papiers* ("without documents" in French) who flirt with deportation and destitution on a daily basis.

Given that civilian fatalities from the war in Afghanistan have been rising, there is a distressing disconnect between reality and the EU response. In an implicit admission of this disconnect, deportations are sometimes paused when a massive terrorist attack takes place in Afghanistan. It is as if European policymakers need reminding that, after all, Afghanistan remains a country steeped in insecurity that claims thousands of lives every year.

None of this is good news for Afghans who are biding their time at the borders of Europe to go for the game. They spend thousands of dollars apiece to embark on an incredibly risky journey. In the process, they are labeled "illegal migrants," an identity that criminalizes them and marks them for exploitation, abuse, and humiliation. "We know this is illegal, we know it is not OK, but we have no other choice," says Jafar. "You must always keep one thing in mind: you will have many difficult moments, you will stay without water, without food, but you have to survive; you have to reach that goal."

After so much expectation, the refugees find a whole new set of hurdles at the destination they have sacrificed so much to reach. Their big challenge will be to convince skeptical authorities that they truly deserve protection. And that might well be the hardest part of all, especially if they are rejected and realize that every struggle has been for nothing.

16

A LIFE IN EXILE

UNDER THE BRIDGE

So many stories start and end in exile. Qammar was born in Pakistan to Afghan parents and lived in a small refugee camp in Swabi District in the northwest, bordering Afghanistan. And yet he did not feel like a refugee: "I had no such feeling. I felt as though I came from there because my father had a job—he sold pots on his bicycle—and I went to school like my younger brother and sisters. I was happy."

One day in 2016, when Qammar was in his late teens, Pakistan made it clear that his family did not belong. Qammar walked home from school with his sister to an appalling sight: "We saw soldiers forcing our family out of our house. We dropped our school bags and rushed over. We were not even allowed to pack our things; we had to leave immediately." The soldiers said they were not allowed to stay in Pakistan any longer and had to go back to their country. The home of Qammar's family was destroyed and their belongings set on fire. The soldiers ordered the bewildered refugees to climb into trucks, drove them to the border with Afghanistan, and waited until they crossed. Qammar says the other residents of the camp met the same fate.

Deportation came as a total surprise to Qammar. "In the morning, you go to school for another regular day of life, and you're already planning for tomorrow. When you come back from school, you must leave everything and go to a completely new country," he recounts. "I cannot describe how I felt then. It was completely abnormal because I had lived all my life in Pakistan, and I was deported to a place that I knew nothing about, even if it was my original country."

Although Qammar did not expect to be deported, Pakistan had been making life increasingly untenable for Afghans within its territory, most of whom had settled after the 1979 Soviet invasion of their homeland. In 2015 there were an estimated 1.5 million registered Afghan refugees and 1 million undocumented Afghans living in Pakistan. But then Pakistan's approach soured, ostensibly because of deteriorating relations with its war-torn neighbor as well as insecurity at least partly blamed on Afghans. Pakistan adopted a counterterrorism plan that included steps to repatriate Afghans, which led to what Human Rights Watch called "the world's largest unlawful mass forced return of refugees in recent times." Pakistani authorities practically forced Afghans out, resorting to a campaign of police abuses, extortion, and deportation threats.

In the case of Qammar's family, the threats were made real. In common with half of the Afghan populations in Pakistan and Iran (Afghanistan's neighbors to the southeast and west, respectively), Qammar was born outside his native country. He had never visited Afghanistan and simply could not imagine what life would be like there. His father did not give him the chance to find out. Qammar explains, "My father worried about me because he lost three brothers in the war in Afghanistan. He decided to send me to Europe, because the same thing could happen to me, and I agreed to leave." Qammar spent only three days in Afghanistan. His father paid a smuggler to take him as far as Turkey. Qammar squatted in an old house in Istanbul and worked twelve hours a day in the city's parks, cleaning them and cutting the grass, for some 350 euros a month.

In Turkey, Qammar soon became aware of his right-less existence as a refugee, just as he had been in Pakistan. Qammar touches the back of his head gingerly as he tells of the time he was robbed after changing his hard-earned savings into euros. "I had four hundred euros and my friend six hundred. Some drunk men attacked us. They hit me with a beer bottle and cut my head and took our money. The police took us to the station, bandaged my head, and told me they could do nothing to help because I had no legal card."

In early 2018, Qammar and some others took advantage of river floods in Turkey's Edirne Province to cross the frontier into Greece. Exploitation and theft followed him. First, he worked on a farm, earn-ing twenty-four euros for eight hours of physical labor, minus three euros automatically deducted by his "employer" for food. Accommodation was free: nine lived in a room used to store farming equipment. Did he get enough to eat? Qammar smiles wanly. "Just for surviving," he replies. After saving enough money for the next move in the game, Qammar moved to Athens, where he immediately bought a new mobile phone. As he walked down the street, talking on his phone, a man drove by on a motorbike and snatched it.

In Athens, Qammar lived under a bridge while he arranged for his trip to Serbia. Although he paid up front for everything, the next smuggler in the chain kidnapped him in Macedonia and demanded more money. "He was not a small man," explains Qammar, referring to the assets—the hideout, men, and dogs—the smuggler had at his disposal. Qammar had to pay up, calling a friend of his back in Greece to whom he had entrusted his savings.

Now in Serbia, Qammar is living under a bridge again. It seems like he is not going anywhere from there. When I ask what he plans to do next, he replies quietly, "What plan? I am under a bridge. I don't have money for the game; I am just hoping I can find some work in Serbia." There is no hope left. "I have no dream. I don't see anything, just I see that the guys who came with me on this journey are all going for the game and some are succeeding. They have gone and I am under the bridge. It's hopeless." Qammar sounds very depressed. I ask if he is still in contact with his family and he shakes his head no. The translator, himself an Afghan refugee, is moved to encourage Qammar by sharing his own difficulties when he first arrived in Serbia two years earlier.

It is no wonder that Qammar has given up. So far, he has spent his young life as an outsider and has been unable to influence his fate. He is not alone in this. Millions of Afghan refugees in Pakistan and Iran find they are no longer welcome. Many will return to Afghanistan, to very real threats posed by destitution and violence, while others will try to go to Europe, as Qammar did. Either way, the odds in their favor are slim.

FATHER AND SON

Jawad had an amazing father. Sadly, the two did not have much time to enjoy each other's company. Jawad never saw Asadulla again after being forced to leave Afghanistan, at the age of thirteen, nearly three decades ago. However, Jawad lives his life as a tribute to his father. He does not say it in so many words, but it is all there in his story: the influence of Asadulla's clear-sighted refusal to condone or to fight in what he called senseless wars, and his efforts to promote education so that others would do likewise. Since Asadulla was born in Afghanistan, he was destined to disappointment and displacement, all the more so because he belonged to a marginalized ethnic group called the Hazara. But at least Asadulla's vision propelled his son to pursue his education in exile in hugely challenging circumstances, and to grow into a wise and gentle man dedicated to helping others.

Today, Jawad lives in Rome with his wife and two children, a long way from Afghanistan's Ghazni Province, where he was born. He turns up to be interviewed in the morning, as scheduled, but we run out of time so he returns in the evening, carrying his five-year-old son. Jawad talks for hours, describing his attempts to escape to Iran in the early 1990s in detail. Our conversation wanders down other channels too. We talk about how religion has the unique potential to connect, although it is so often exploited to divide, and about being receptive to the surprises that life springs on us. "We have to be ready to receive, to welcome what comes. This means that we need to be open to what is good and beautiful in this life. There are many bad things but also beautiful ones," says Jawad. He leans forward to stroke his sleeping son's face and to kiss him before taking up the thread of the conversation again.

Jawad knows something about the bad things in life, not only those that befell him personally, but also the heavy heritage of the ethnic group he was born into. He starts his story by digging into history, going back to the late nineteenth century, when the Hazara population was decimated under the rule of Afghanistan's Abdur Rahman Khan. Abdur Rahman declared war on the Hazara, whom he had designated as unbelievers, because most are Shia rather than Sunni Muslims. It is estimated that 60 percent of the Hazara were killed in the emir's brutal campaign. Tens of thousands were enslaved while others fled as refugees to India and Pakistan. Their lands were confiscated. Persecution and humiliation followed the Hazara through the decades; they were seen and treated as second-class citizens. The Taliban also pursued them relentlessly, perpetuating mass killings and deliberately seeking to destroy their cultural identity.

It was to promote the development of the Hazara that Jawad's father set up an association in rural Ghazni in the 1970s. Initially, things went well, and the association started a clinic and a school. However, Asadulla had no control over fast-moving events in Afghanistan. The country slid into civil war, with the Soviet-backed government on one side and Islamic militias known as *mujahedin* on the other, indirectly supported by the United States. Hazara groups were drawn into the conflict, sometimes fighting one another. When the association set up by Asadulla morphed into an armed group, he withdrew. Jawad recalls, "He said our aim was not to go to senseless war between brothers. His real brother belonged to a rival group."

Due to his refusal to get involved, Asadulla had to leave the land where he had always lived, as his fathers had done before him. He took his family to Helmand Province and got a job as a civil servant. Jawad was a toddler at the time. Seven years passed before war caught up with the family again. The government called up all men aged twenty to forty-five to fight against the *mujahedin*. Once again, Asadulla declined to take up arms. "My father said it was impossible to fight for the Russians against the people of Afghanistan," explains Jawad. "He said he had left his place not to go into senseless war and he would not get involved now." The government ordered house-to-house searches to round up those men who did not come forward. Asadulla hid in the cellar under piles of wooden logs. When night fell, he went back to Ghazni and dispatched his own father to collect his wife and children.

In Ghazni, Asadulla found the same threat of forced conscription waiting for him, this time at the request of the Hazara militia controlling the area. Despite his protestations, Asadulla was not allowed to remain neutral. He reached a compromise, persuading the militia to accept regular donations of the grain he cultivated. The grain pacified the militia until Jawad was thirteen years old, at which point they said he should join their ranks because he was old enough to carry a gun. Jawad pauses in his story to add a quick aside: "Still today, there are many child soldiers who kill and are killed in Afghanistan. The armed groups use minors a lot."

Thanks to Asadulla, the young Jawad could already think critically about the chaos in his country: "My father was very wise and far-sighted. He always told us stories to explain the mess in Afghanistan, what was going on, and who was fighting who." Jawad even recognized that sometimes "you don't understand which side you are on and why you are fighting." When the summons from the militia came, Asadulla asked his son to decide for himself. Jawad replied, "Just as you did not want to fight in a senseless war, I don't want to either." Either way, Asadulla knew his son was lost to him: "If you don't go with them, you can no longer stay in Afghanistan. You choose: you go with them or you leave the country."

"MAKE IT OR DIE"

Jawad left Afghanistan with his cousin, who faced the same predicament. They went first to Pakistan and found a smuggler to take them across the border to Iran. Jawad tells how they were taken in the middle of the desert and ordered to climb into a pickup truck: "There were three or four smugglers, each with a stick in hand. They counted *one, two, three!* At the count of three, we had to sit down together, and if someone did not, they hit him on the head with the stick." Jawad describes the desert as "all sand and only sand. Sand is always in movement, with the wind. If today you see a dune here, tomorrow it moves there—that's sand for you."

The pickup left Jawad and his companions in the middle of nowhere and they crossed "many mountains" in the dark of night. They were robbed on the way. "We were in a valley, and we saw thieves climbing down both sides, holding torches and pointing guns at us. They told us to give them everything we had of value in our pockets: money, watches, rings, whatever. We even left new jackets and shoes there," Jawad says. The refugees did not dare to keep anything back because the bandits threatened to bind them and leave them in the valley if they disobeyed. Jawad suffered a practically painful loss: "In Quetta, everyone was saying that we would cross the mountains, so I bought new gym shoes. The thieves took my shoes and left me with bare feet. I had a change of clothes in my bag and I tore them and bandaged my feet with the strips. There were thorns in the path and my feet bled badly." To this day, Jawad carries the scars on his feet to remind him of that trek, which ultimately turned out to be futile.

In the early hours of morning, still under cover of darkness, the group arrived on level ground in Iranian territory and started running toward waiting pickups. Jawad gripped his cousin's hand and they quickened their pace just as the Iranian border guards appeared. Jawad thinks they were alerted by the sound of so many footsteps; he estimates there were about three hundred people in the group.

A nightmarish scene followed. "It was a very ugly moment that I will never forget, that night, because the police started firing and people were screaming and crying," Jawad recalls. The refugees crowded around the pickups, trying to climb in. The drivers wanted to escape and ran over many of them. Jawad says the worst thing was that at least two men lost a leg in the mayhem. "It happened like this: they were climbing into the pickup when it started to move, and so they had one leg in and one leg out. The pickup dragged them a long way, because one leg was trapped inside by the people, who were already sitting on each other. They didn't manage to pull the leg free and so it was torn off. They screamed and screamed; it was ugly, ugly."

Jawad was one of those who did not manage to jump into a pickup. The guards put the remaining refugees in five rows, with pickup trucks surrounding them left and right, front and back, and told them to run. The men and boys ran for more than two hours in the desert. When any one of them faltered, a pickup hit him. Jawad made it only thanks to his cousin: "He was stronger than me, and he dragged me."

The refugees were allowed to sleep off their exhaustion in soldiers' barracks. The next day, hungry and thirsty, they were told there was nothing for them. The guards pointed to a pile of moldy bread, leftovers that had begun to rot. They said, "If you want bread, there it is; eat that." The refugees swore they would not touch the bread, "not even if we died of hunger. Not even an animal could eat it." To slake their thirst, there was only undrinkable salty water. When the night chill fell, the guards refused to give them blankets, and during the heat of the day, they forced the refugees to sit in the sun.

Jawad laughs a bit when he says this, as he does for the more unpalatable parts of his story. It is not that he finds what he is saying amusing but rather derisory in some way. He says, "It was to punish us because we were *clandestini* [clandestine]. We must never think again of coming to Iran. So we spent three days like this, in the sun, in the cold, without eating. I just lay there, stretched out. I couldn't even talk." On the fourth day, what had seemed unthinkable on the first day became possible. "When darkness fell, I heard someone chewing something crunchy. I told my cousin, 'Someone must have found food.'" One of them had succumbed and was eating the moldy bread. "Suddenly, we all rushed to the pile of bread and devoured it."

The following day was unsurprisingly a disaster. All very ill, Jawad and his companions were transferred to another camp, where they were registered prior to deportation. Jawad says: "We signed a letter to state we would never dream of coming to Iran ever again and that, if we did, we could be killed. Very well, we signed everything." The next day, he was loaded into a truck and returned to Afghanistan. While they recovered in a hut in the desert that catered to deportees like them, Jawad and his cousin decided to try to go to Iran again. Why? The answer is simple: "Because we could not go back to Afghanistan." They were not short of choice when it came to choosing a smuggler. "Many smugglers come and make offers, saying this or that way is safe. Then you decide with whom you should go."

The two cousins opted for the most dangerous route because it was quickest: directly from Afghanistan to Iran across a heavily mined border. "We had been warned never to try to go that way because we would surely die. But, after what we had just been through, we decided that it was better to die once than to die every day. It no longer mattered. We couldn't go back, so we'd try: make it or die." Consciously playing with metaphor, Jawad explains their state of mind at the time: "We had reached the end of the road. Enough! We were tired."

This time, the refugee group was smaller because the journey promised to be so dangerous. At the mountains at the border, they received chilling instructions from the smugglers: "Go in a single file, and put one foot exactly in front of the other, without making a mistake. Otherwise, you'll fall into the valley, because the path is so rocky, or step on a mine and blow up in the air." The journey was undertaken in pitch darkness, and the remains of those who had tried before and failed haunted them. Jawad remembers, "I grabbed the shirt of the person in front of me because we could not see nothing. We could smell the stench of bodies of those who had fallen in the valley below. We saw their bones." Nothing befell the group because "we were very good, we respected all their rules, and we arrived safe," and no one arrested them on the Iranian side of the border.

"TRY TO STUDY"

The boys' ultimate destination was the city of Isfahan, a favorite of Afghan refugees because, according to Jawad, there were many factories where "even a *clandestino* without papers could find work, see?" Reaching Isfahan took about ten days of cautious travel in the smugglers' bus. Once the group arrived, the smugglers took Jawad hostage because he was the youngest, to make sure they got paid. The rest went to borrow money from fellow Afghans, which they did within days. Jawad and his cousin found work in a marble factory and labored for two years to settle their debts. Jawad hardly ever ventured out because he was afraid of being caught in Iran illegally. "Anyone who had a police uniform, I was afraid of," he says. Jawad worked nonstop, seventeen hours every day of the week. His industriousness meant that he saved money to send home.

It was then that Jawad received a letter from his father that would change the course of his life. Jawad no longer has the letter but remembers the words as if he read them yesterday: "My son, I did not send you away from home so that you would remain ignorant. You know only too well how I fought to educate others and that a big part of Afghanistan's problem, of people who go to war for nothing, is ignorance. Ignorance has created many problems for our society, for us. Now that you are far from this country full of problems, I hope you will find some way to study. Try to study. I don't want money from you. Yes, I like money, just as everyone does, but I have not been well off at any time in my life, and I don't want to live off yours. I am working the land and managing to look after the family. Don't worry about us."

Jawad starts to cry as he recites the words of Asadulla, even more so when he tells me that his father died the previous year. "It was like an order from my father, no? That I should study?" he asks me. This is what the young Jawad understood and he immediately tried to start studying. But it was easier said than done. "There were two big obstacles before me. One was that I had no documents and I was afraid even to go out of the factory. The other was that refugees were not enrolled in school in Iran then." Again, Jawad inserts a bracket in his story: "This is still a problem in Iran, although things have changed a bit."

Jawad persevered until he found a solution. A friend proposed that Jawad join a madrassah (Islamic school) so that the school administration would formally recommend that he get his papers. This is exactly what happened. Within a year, Iran had recognized Jawad as a refugee, and he embarked on years of studying not only in the madrassah but also in night school. He graduated in mathematics and sociology and went on to get a master's in history.

Still, life was far from perfect. Jawad may have obtained his papers and advanced in his studies, but he could only get so far. He explains, "Even if you are 'legal,' you cannot get a job that is worthy of you in Iran. All the work I did in Iran was illegal, without a contract, without rights, nothing, nothing, nothing, total exploitation, like a slave, a miserable life." Jawad did all kinds of manual labor to survive. "I worked every summer and accepted any work. The first day of the school holidays, I would start to work."

Eighteen years passed, during which time Jawad met the woman who would become his wife. A Hazara from Afghanistan like him, she was studying in Italy, and they met when she came to visit her sister in Iran. After getting married, they moved together to Italy, where Jawad was granted asylum. His first job was delivering pizza by *motorino* (a small motorcycle ubiquitous on Italy's streets). Then he heard about a master's program in religion and cultural mediation at Sapienza University in Rome. Jawad has just graduated from this program and works as a cultural mediator. His wife, who has graduate degrees in biochemistry and chemical engineering, does the same kind of work he does.

HAPPY IN ROME

"We are happy in Rome because we have full rights: the right to study, to work, and to live a normal life, which we did not have in Afghanistan or in Iran," says Jawad. "And I am happy because we are safe." But there is a cloud on Jawad's horizon: the inflammatory anti-immigrant rhetoric and policies of the Italian government that ruled for much of 2018 and 2019. "Let's hope for the best," he says.

Jawad's approach to life is the antithesis of the xenophobic hostility displayed by populist politicians. As I understand it, his premise is that we cannot appreciate what life has to offer if we remain locked in our own bubble of sameness. He puts it like this: "There are many things to know, to discover in this wonderful world. All cultures have beautiful aspects, just as different kinds of flowers in the garden are uniquely beautiful. So far, we don't have much hope of seeing all this beauty. Perhaps one day we will."

The message of Jawad has been molded by a lifetime of suffering, by the wisdom inherited from his father, and by years of diligent study. He is doing his utmost to spread this message in a way that is unassuming but still compelling. Jawad's hopes for his son, like those Asadulla had for him, are worth remembering: that he will have the opportunity to study and to grow in knowledge and to appreciate the beauty of the garden of the world.

Part III

Destination?

17

SAFE FOR NOW

"BEAUTIFUL BUT SO EXPENSIVE"

"Our daughter is always saying she wants to die, to be with her uncle, and that she wants to kill herself somehow." Mustafa and Asma are extremely worried about their daughter, Fatima. After seeing the dead body of her favorite uncle, Wael, on ghastly display in the street, the little girl withdrew into her own grief-stricken world. Her overwhelming sadness persisted even after the family escaped from Raqqa and the cruel control of ISIS, who had killed Wael. Three years later, when I visit the family in Beirut, nine-year-old Fatima has yet to recover.

The couple cannot afford to get professional help—they struggle just to put food on the table every day—but humanitarian aid pays for Fatima's treatment. She feels better after the sessions with her psychologist, but the downside is that the medication she takes makes her drowsy, so that she spends much of her time sleeping instead of going to school. Worry about Fatima and her crippling condition tops a long list of anxieties that Mustafa and his wife face every day.

As refugees in Lebanon, theirs is a plight carefully measured in statistics and revealed to be precarious at best. In 2018, two-thirds of the refugees were classified as officially poor, and many lived in garages, tents, warehouses, or cattle sheds because they could not afford to pay steep rent for tiny apartments. Most could not meet their food and health-care costs. More than half of Syrian refugee children in Lebanon were out of school. The older they were, the higher the percentage. This is hardly to be wondered at: an estimated 1.5 million Syrians have sought refuge in their small neighboring country, which means that one out of every five people living in Lebanon is now a Syrian refugee. Most do not have legal residency because they cannot afford to pay the $200 annual fee or the obligatory Lebanese sponsor.

Mustafa, Asma, and their five children feature in this depressing list of statistics. At least they can afford an apartment—just. They pay $350 a month, an exorbitant sum given that neither parent holds a fixed job. Mustafa grimaces when we talk about the rent: "The landlord comes on the very day the rent is due; he will not wait even two or three days. He tells us, 'If you can't give it to me now, get out!'"

Mustafa takes on casual labor when he can, but he has not found anything for weeks. It is more difficult for Mustafa than some: because ISIS flogged him in Raqqa, his back still hurts and he cannot do heavy work such as construction, one of the mainstays of employment for refugees in Lebanon. "I wish I could earn enough for my kids," he says. But it is impossible in these circumstances. So his eleven-year-old son must work in a barber's shop as well as go to school. In sum, Mustafa and Asma find Beirut "beautiful but so expensive" and reminiscence with nostalgia about their beloved Raqqa.

"EVERYONE HAS A STORY"

Hibah, who left Aleppo as soon as the bombings reached her neighborhood, tried returning to Syria. Strange as it may seem, Hibah went back to seek medical answers for the seemingly mysterious condition of her son, who was born in Beirut. She recalls, "My baby was sick for six months and losing weight all this time. The doctor said the medicine was not working and not to bring him anymore because there was nothing to be done." In despair, Hibah decided in 2013 to take her son to Syria, where hospital care was free of charge.

Just as leaving Syria during the war posed challenges, going back was tricky. Hibah had entered Lebanon via a smuggling route. If she wanted to leave Lebanon through a legal border crossing, Hibah would have to pay a $400 fine for being unregistered. She sold her fridge, wardrobe, and washing machine and got $200. Her brother gave her $200, and friends contributed another $200, so she had enough for travel costs too. Hibah's gamble paid off. She took her son to a hospital in northwest

Syria and they discovered that he was suffering an adverse reaction to milk. Hibah stayed in Syria for two years before returning to Beirut, because her husband had stayed back, fearing forced conscription.

Back in Beirut, her children's health problems continue to stress Hibah. Her daughter was diagnosed as diabetic when she was seven. Hibah and her husband have fallen into debt to pay for regular insulin injections and blood tests. He installs gypsum for a living but has been out of work for months. On the brink of tears, Hibah talks about the losing battle to cover her children's medical bills and about how exhausted she gets, coming and going to the UN office for refugees to beg for help. A glance at her apartment shows how hard Hibah works to keep things together. The place is spotless. Blankets are stacked neatly in one corner and precise rows of plastic jars with lentils, beans, other legumes, and rice line the shelves in the miniscule kitchen next door. A colorful children's bicycle is parked in a corner.

Hibah herself sits on a mat on the living room floor, surrounded by cushions. She wears a fluffy bright pink top, with a green blanket draped over, and leans against a crimson curtain. A scarf is pulled tightly over her head such that her lovely but worried features are accentuated more prominently against the medley of color. I ask about friends. For the first time, Hibah smiles faintly, and replies drily, "I have friends, and they are all worse off than I am. Everyone has a story." Her friends are Syrian, in common with the other refugees I meet in Lebanon, such as Zainab, who left Raqqa because she was afraid that ISIS would abduct her son. Zainab says she found great help from her compatriots in exile: "When we cook, we share food. When the others know I cannot buy bread, they bring for me. When we could not pay the rent, they made a collection and paid for us."

STRAINED HOSPITALITY

In a country with so many refugees and a high unemployment rate, imagine how hard it must be to find work. It is not clear what the unemployment rate is: in 2017, Lebanon's labor minister put it at 25 percent, rising sharply among youth. Less than a year later, Lebanon's president pitched it at 46 percent. The official rate is 10 percent, dating back to 2012. Refugees are blamed for high unemployment and are vulnerable to exploitation, especially if they are unregistered, reflecting a global reality.

When Salma's husband persuaded her to come to Lebanon because he had found work in a biscuit factory, she thought it sounded like a safe bet. Although her husband's prospective employers sponsored the family to come to Lebanon legally, they refused to pay him once he started working. Salma says indignantly, "They told my husband that if he did not work for them, he would have to go back to Syria, because they were his sponsors." To add insult to injury, the employers gave the family a house that was completely empty. "We put shoes to use as pillows and covered ourselves with our clothes to sleep," continues Salma. "I started crying and said I wanted to go back to Syria."

Instead, the family moved to Beirut, where they are managing to get by. As I go from one tiny apartment to another, some with more furniture and facilities than others, depending on individual fortunes, a picture of poverty emerges. In one small room, rented by a family of six, the mother waves her hand around: "Look, the bathroom, kitchen, and bedroom, all in here." Ah, the bathroom! I was wondering what was behind the crumpled brown curtain hanging floor to ceiling, dragged across a tiny space in the corner. The mark of poverty is evident not only in cramped spaces and dilapidated apartment blocks, but also in worried faces, most of all when parents talk about rent and medical fees.

Adding to the hardship of Syrian refugees in Lebanon is the hostility they sometimes meet. Although Lebanon has been incredibly hospitable, to the extent of introducing double shifts in its schools to accommodate refugee children in the afternoon, public attitudes do not always follow suit. Some Lebanese students bully and fight with their Syrian peers between the shifts. Some Lebanese parents threaten to remove their children from public schools hosting refugees and to enroll them elsewhere, because they do not want their children to sit at the same desks as Syrian children.

At a wider level, there is a disturbing trend of actual or threatened evictions of Syrian refugees in some municipalities in Lebanon. There are many stated reasons: for example, that the refugees' informal settlements are illegal and a source of pollution. The government is also clamping down on so-called semi-permanent structures, the small concrete shelters or cement-enhanced tents that refugees erect in their settlements.

With rising tensions, any spark can light a flame. This is what happened in one refugee camp in the Bekaa Valley in Lebanon in June 2019, when an accidental fire led to an altercation between the refugees and a firefighter, which in turn provoked the eviction of six hundred refugees who were attacked by vigilante groups. The writing on the wall is worryingly reminiscent of a campaign in Pakistan a few years ago that forced Afghan refugees out, among them Qammar, by creating an environment of hostility that made life so unbearable for the refugees that they returned home, albeit unwillingly.

There are many possible reasons for the hostility. Some are geopolitical and historical, like decades of Syrian domination of Lebanon that ended in 2005. Others are more current: some political factions scapegoat the refugees for Lebanon's deteriorating economy, and many Lebanese have come to see the huge population of refugees as a burden. They echo the alarm of their prime minister, Saad Hariri, who has said that their country is being turned into "one big refugee camp."

Of course, not all Lebanese resent the presence of the refugees. Zainab says reasonably, "Some Lebanese are friendly and others are not." She admits that some insult her in the streets of her neighborhood in Beirut: "They tell us to go away, back to Syria, that we are ruining Lebanon and making it dirty." But she is quick to add that others are kind, stopping her in the street to chat, usually about her little girls. "They tell me my daughters are very pretty and they open up the conversation," she says. "They ask us how we lived, what happened to us, and what is life like here."

"AT LEAST WE ARE SAFE HERE"

For most refugees who are trying their best to start over, life in Lebanon is hugely challenging because it does not really give them the opportunity to do so. They can barely afford daily life. One Iraqi woman I meet for a few minutes puts it well. Almost as soon as she starts to talk, her sunny smile gives way to tears. "We lost everything, everything!" she sobs. When ISIS overran her home city of Mosul, they gave her family minutes to get out. They ran out of their home barefooted, with just the clothes they wore. The woman says she is tired of crying and wants to start a new life, but Beirut is too expensive, so she wants to go somewhere else, anywhere. Her other ambition is to keep smiling for her children so they will be happy. In this, Lebanon has been good for them: her children smile all the time here because they feel safe. In the space of a few minutes, this unforgettable woman manages to say everything that is essential—and to recover her dazzling smile by the end of it.

Something in what she says rings universally true: Lebanon is safe, at least for now. Yes, most of the refugees are poor, and they miss the comparative luxury of their life in prewar Syria, but there is no deadly danger. This is one message I hear consistently as the refugees muse with mixed feelings. Zainab says, "Back in Syria, I had a house and a garden, with chickens, sheep, and goats. We made cheese and *labneh*. We had land to cultivate cotton, and we grew grapes and pomegranates, everything healthy." No more words are necessary. Zainab's present-day bleak surroundings speak volumes after the rosy picture she has just painted. "Here, I don't have all this, but I have peace of mind. Sometimes I do worry, because I cannot provide for my kids what they need, but we are safe at least. Just not seeing my son kidnapped by ISIS is enough for me. At least here I can see him grow and get an education."

Mariam is content in Lebanon. Her husband worked as an electrician in Beirut for years before she joined him, and her apartment is better furnished than the others I see, with china ornaments lining the shelves, a big flat-screen television, and an air-conditioning unit. She says, "It's true Syria was home, but either a bomb or ISIS could have destroyed us, and they kidnapped my boy. Now I put my head on the pillow and I sleep safely."

Research indicates that Syrian refugees remain deeply reluctant, at best, to return home unless they have guarantees of physical safety and economic survival and can return to the specific places they left—all conditions that remain in the realms of fantasy at this time. Although the Assad regime is calling on refugees to return and has consolidated control over most of Syria, thanks to Iranian and Russian help, more than 1.5 million Syrians fled their homes in 2018. In 2019, Syrian and Russian warplanes relentlessly continued to bombard civilian targets, including hospitals, in the last rebel-held enclave in Idlib in the north.

An urgent appeal by rescue workers, medics, and humanitarians in the zone said, "We are devastated that the world has turned its back on us."

There is not much to go home to. With the collapse of rule of law in Syria, arbitrary arrests and detention, abductions, and disappearances have become commonplace, perpetrated by criminal gangs, armed groups, and regime forces. Far from decreasing, the rate of arrests and executions has been increasing. Many fear reprisals if they return. Widespread apprehension lingers about Syria's mandatory military conscription, which countless men left the country to avoid in the first place. Homes have either been destroyed or occupied by others who were displaced within Syria. Even with an intact and vacant home waiting for them, some refugees still utterly reject the idea of going back, with a fear that borders on abhorrence. They have seen too much, suffered too much. Picking up where they left off is not an option.

18

THE DANGERS OF WAITING

WASTED TIME

In another corner of the world, in northern Ethiopia, a young man called Fanuel has lived alone in a remote refugee camp for five years and longs with all his heart to go to Europe. So far, fear of the journey holds Fanuel back, because he has heard about human traffickers who harvest organs. But it is touch and go: Fanuel is so tired of waiting to get on with his life that I would not be surprised to hear one day that he has left, in dangerous defiance of fate.

"Yeah," he says thoughtfully, "I still think about Europe because there is no other option. I'm worried about my future. I cannot build my future here and I've wasted enough time. I've lived all these years for nothing; I accomplished nothing. Sometimes, I can't control my emotions. I just feel like going somewhere but I'm afraid I will lose my life. That's the problem that has kept me sitting here, because I want to leave."

Fanuel lives just across the border from his homeland of Eritrea, which he left five years ago, after being called up to serve in the military. Aware of the open-ended nature of this "invitation," Fanuel did what countless Eritrean youth have done before him: he escaped to Ethiopia and settled in one of several refugee camps set up by the Ethiopian government in the north. He took off alone when he was eighteen, leaving behind his mother and three sisters in abject poverty, which broke his heart.

In his soft-spoken and precise manner, Fanuel explains how he felt as a new arrival in the refugee camp, and how quickly the pendulum swung from hope to despair. "I was lost in my life, because I had dreams in Eritrea that I would get somewhere I could feel free and safe and work like a citizen. But then nothing came true. My dreams couldn't come true, because there is nothing to do in the camp. I cannot improve my life. I don't know what's going to be my future. I thank God that I'm still alive."

If Fanuel decides to leave Ethiopia, he knows he may not remain alive for much longer. Young refugees leave the camps in droves to head for Europe, usually via the deadly Central Mediterranean route. Despair seems to be catching in the camps, which are located in geographical spaces that are beautiful but remote and bare, with minimal employment and higher educational opportunities. Time hangs heavily and daily life for the majority is a struggle for survival.

Many if not most of the refugees live for resettlement to a more affluent country, but this golden privilege is available to only 1 percent of refugees globally and is becoming increasingly elusive. The United States, once the most welcoming country in the world in terms of resettlement, has drastically reduced its Refugee Admissions Program in recent years. An elderly refugee told me that youth sometimes shout incessantly through the night. "Why? For nothing. They are depressed and frustrated. It's like waiting for something that never happens." Fanuel, who is translating the conversation, resonates with this. Later, he exclaims, "It's like the old man said: waiting for something that is never going to happen."

The scenario could well improve in Ethiopia because the government passed a progressive refugee law in early 2019. One of the provisions allows refugees to work. Ethiopia is a very generous host, offering shelter to close to one million refugees who have fled conflict in neighboring countries, chief among them South Sudan and Eritrea. This law goes one step further, but it will not solve all the problems: work in Ethiopia will probably remain hard to come by, even when refugees can search for it legally, and leaving the camp will mean losing subsistence rations and free shelter, however basic. Time will tell what difference the new law makes.

HOW TO STOP WORRYING

Meanwhile, Fanuel has adjusted to camp life. "I accepted it mentally," he says. He credits a book with turning around his attitude: the self-help classic by Dale Carnegie, *How to Stop Worrying and Start Living*. I am both delighted and surprised when he says this—delighted because, as a chronic worrier, I love that particular book, and surprised at the extent to which it has leapt across cultural, situational, and temporal boundaries with its messages about positive and commonsense thinking. It turns out that Fanuel loves to read and has devoured all the books in a small library that an NGO set up in the camp.

Self-help titles are his firm favorite because they have given him confidence and help him to manage his worries, "so I can pull myself up." I ask Fanuel what he remembers most from the Carnegie book. He replies promptly, "How to cooperate with something you can't change. Then there are some techniques that really work—for example, how to banish worries. You have to ask yourself, 'What am I worrying about, what can I do about it, and what is the best solution?' and like that. First analyze the problem. That is really helpful."

Two years ago, Fanuel got a job in the camp as a para-counselor with an NGO, after excelling in short training courses. The stipend is low but the job has given Fanuel an interest in life. Actually, it is not so much the job itself as the opportunity to help others. "If I see people suffering, I just feel something really bad I can't control," he says. "So, helping people is really what makes me happy; there is nothing like that. We are here on this earth only for a short time. We have to help each other."

Something else that made a big difference to Fanuel's slow and solitary life in exile was meeting his mother again after more than five years. Due to the repressive regime in Eritrea and the poverty of his family, the two could not communicate after his departure. Their joyful reunion was made possible in 2018 by an agreement between Ethiopia and Eritrea to make peace after decades of hostility. Almost as soon as the border between the two countries reopened, relatives of the refugees flooded across from Eritrea to join them in the camps, or just to visit. Fanuel says excitedly, "I was really worried about my mother, but now I am almost OK, because I saw her face. At least I came to realize that she is still OK." He stresses the word *saw*, and his face cracks into a big smile. His mother came with a neighbor and they stayed for two days before returning to Eritrea, where Fanuel's sisters still live.

Fanuel hopes they will be together again, someday, somewhere. This is partly why he is so preoccupied about his future. He says with a sense of urgency, "I want to help my family, especially my mother, who brought me up. I can never pay back what she did for me but at least I could help a little. I want to *do* something, to get work and to build my life like other people, to own a house, which I can call mine." Fanuel's dreams are nothing out of the ordinary—we all share them—but attaining them is much harder for some than for others. Such is Fanuel's lot. So far, he is "waiting to see what tomorrow brings" and has managed to rein in expectation while keeping hope alive. God willing, things will turn out right for Fanuel and his hope will not drive him to decisions he might not live to regret.

THINK TWICE

Contrary to Fanuel, Isaias is thrilled to live in a refugee camp in Ethiopia, because he descended into hell when he tried to leave. Isaias is one of the unfortunates who wound up in an underground torture cell in the Sinai Desert in Egypt at the mercy of notoriously evil traffickers who held him for ransom. He returned to Ethiopia after a six-month ordeal. "For me, it is like a good and special thing to live here in Ethiopia, because I have seen the worst there," Isaias assures me. "When I returned here, I was so happy, because I found people who talked my language and understood me."

Isaias feels duty bound to warn other refugees, like Fanuel, who are dying to leave for Europe: "Think twice or more. You have to understand what is going on there; get information from everyone who is talking about it. Don't be rash. Don't decide impulsively."

Slight in build and soft spoken, Isaias can now recount his real-life nightmare calmly, but it was not always this way. Humanitarian agencies in the camp eagerly encourage those like Isaias to share their testimony to dissuade others from falling into the same lethal trap. At first, Isaias used to break down in tears in public because he relived the torture when he talked about it. Still, he persevered: "I have no choice because I want to teach people. I want to tell them the truth. I don't want them to go there."

Isaias himself left Eritrea in 2009, after being recruited to the army at age seventeen and serving nearly two years. He escaped when he was assigned to the border with Ethiopia, and he spent a year in a refugee camp before leaving for Sudan with some friends. Isaias attributes this decision to "misinformation" from other Eritreans in Sudan. The smugglers who took Isaias and his friends to Sudan cheated them, promising that they were headed for Khartoum but sending them to the Sinai instead. "Once we arrived in Sudan, they changed the plan, blindfolded and kept us in some hiding place," recalls Isaias. The kidnapped boys were sold to Egyptian traffickers who took them to an underground prison cell, where they were ordered to bring $33,000 each for their release.

Isaias shudders when he remembers what happened next: "We said we could not pay so much money. We were new, we did not know the situation, so we thought they would understand. They chose two of us at random and killed them in front of us, smashing their head with an iron bar. They made it clear we would be next if we did not get the money." The prisoners were kept blindfolded and chained to one another, their hands and legs bound. Sometimes they did not eat or drink for three days at a stretch. Six of the group died there and, at the time, Isaias envied them. "We really wanted to die because it would have been a big relief," he admits. "Every time they tortured us, we were sure we would die that day. Our wounds just grew and grew and got infected."

The cruelty of the torture inflicted on refugees in the Sinai dungeons is notorious. Echoing the testimony of many others, Isaias says he was hung from the ceiling from his wrists or arms, so his feet dangled off the floor. He was beaten with metal rods, seared with burning iron on his back, and given electric shocks. Isaias was tormented by the suffering of the others, too, especially the women, whose experience was "really horrible even to imagine." Typically, the torturers called the relatives of their victims, so that they could hear the screams and make haste to send the ransom.

Isaias was one of the last to leave. He spent three months in that hellhole and was released only after his family paid up, which they sold their home and all their cattle in Eritrea to do. Isaias was thrown into the desert and arrested by Egyptian police for being in the country illegally. He was kept in custody for three months, and his wounds were treated, before being returned to Ethiopia.

When Isaias went back to the camp, it seemed like heaven to him. He benefited from intensive counseling, took a course in basic counseling skills himself, and slowly began to move on. When we meet, six years down the line, he says with a shy smile that he has just gotten married. He has also been granted the keenly sought-after opportunity to resettle in the United States. Determined as ever to share his experience, Isaias is gratified that it will be published: "Please share my story all over the world because such things should not happen again."

Today, Isaias comes across as a serene young man, at peace with himself and with his decision to use his life as an example for others. The value of his testimony lies in urging his peers to learn from his mistakes. He teaches another lesson too: that you can suffer the tortures of the damned and yet overcome.

"NOW IT IS TIME TO LIVE"

Nabeel bubbles with positive energy. He says it is because he is *living* now; before, he was just surviving. This motif runs through his eager description of the joy of life now compared to the monotony of before, when he hid from terrorists in his native Pakistan and then sweated in limbo as a refugee in Sri Lanka. Twenty-four-year-old Nabeel is resettled in San Diego, California, an opportunity that surely makes him the envy of millions of refugees around the world. Not that Nabeel's life is easy or luxurious in any way. San Diego is an expensive place to live and Nabeel is working hard at a full-time job as a hotel receptionist and part-time as a barista to make ends meet. When he has time, he goes to classes, to finish secondary school, because he could not do so back home.

For Nabeel, this demanding schedule is just fine because he is *doing* something, not just sitting around. He is busy catching up with life, making up for lost time. "You have a lot of things to do here," he says when we meet in a resettlement office in San Diego. "You have to work, you have to pay rent, and you have to struggle. It's definitely way, way better than waiting, not doing anything." Today, Nabeel feels pretty good about himself: "I'm twenty-four. I feel very accomplished. It's

been a year since I came to the US and I've got me a car, I'm independent, and I go to classes. I have family members who look up to me;
they are proud of me for being here."

Nabeel's sense of fulfilment comes from the power of contrast. He
knows what it feels like to be confined in a physical and mental sense by
the decisions and actions of others. Like Jawad from Afghanistan, Nabeel is a member of the Hazara minority, which faces discrimination in
Pakistan too. He explains, "We are half a million living in Quetta. This
city is known to be very dangerous because of the high number of
terrorist attacks in the last decade. Most were aimed at our community." Pakistani militant groups target the Hazara because they are on
the opposite side of the Muslim divide: the Hazara are mostly Shia
while Pakistan is mostly Sunni.

While the attacks are part of anti-Shia violence across Pakistan, the
Hazara in Quetta are especially vulnerable because "we are distinctive;
we have a different language and different facial features," says Nabeel.
The terrorist attacks have forced the Hazara to confine themselves to
two neighborhoods in the city. To leave these virtual ghettoes is to risk
their lives, and so they steer clear of going to work, to school, to university, just about anywhere. Even so, losses have been heavy. "Every
street, every neighbor, everyone has a story to tell of who they lost,
either friend or family, in those terrorist attacks," Nabeel says. "There is
no one from our people, that you ask them if they lost someone, and
their answer is no."

Nabeel could not wait to leave. He had no immediate family to hold
him back. His parents and siblings were dead, so he decided to try to
reach Australia via Sri Lanka together with his aunt and cousins. They
applied for asylum in Sri Lanka and received a positive response quite
quickly. That was the easy part. Then tedium set in. Nabeel recalls,
"The hard part of Sri Lanka was that we were not allowed to work or
study. Not doing anything, just waiting." The resettlement process took
four long years. There was no option to go to Australia, where Nabeel
had relatives and friends from the Quetta Hazara community, so he
waited to be sent elsewhere.

With nothing to break the monotony of enforced idleness, Nabeel
lived in fervent anticipation of "something so precious" to come. Time
ground to a halt. "When you are not doing anything, time just doesn't go
by; you are just waiting. The worst part is that once you go for your

interview, it takes them weeks, months, even a year to respond." Nabeel describes how he obsessed about his application because he had nothing better to do: "You wake up, that's all you think about; you go to sleep, that's all you think about: what's going to happen? Every time the phone rings or vibrates, like, 'It's them! It's them!' It messes with your mind. Eventually, you just lose motivation. You lose the desire to do anything with life. You just wake up, go to sleep, eat, the same thing. By the time you get resettled, you don't care about anything anymore."

"YOU REALIZE IT'S NOT A FAIRY TALE"

At long last, the moment came, "a very good experience" greeted with both happiness and apprehension: "What were we getting ourselves into?" Nabeel feels they "got lucky" when they were resettled in San Diego. Expensive it might be, and tough to find a job, too, but what matters most to Nabeel is that he can make his own way now. He's on his own and he loves it. He explains why: "In Sri Lanka, for four years I looked to friends and family to support me financially, because I wasn't allowed to work. Someone *has* to support you. Just the *feeling* of not depending on someone else . . . I can't express it in words. It's an amazing feeling." Even better, Nabeel is now in a position to help others back in Pakistan. "I am fortunate to help those left behind. I understand that people in my circles may need help because of the situation there, and from time to time I do help them, and it makes me feel accomplished."

Nabeel did not set his expectations high when he came to the United States: "I wasn't expecting much. I mean there's no competition between me and someone who is living here their whole life, to get a job in a field like business or engineering. I hadn't been to school for years and I wasn't a very good student in the first place." He is going to school now, thanks to a resettlement program that helps young refugees to complete high school at their own pace. Nabeel admits it is "not the best" to work and study at the same time, but he is trying anyway, "to keep up with everything, and maybe eventually it will lead to something." He puts it all down to the worthy cause of pursuing his dreams.

Proud as Nabeel is of the material accomplishments that have allowed him to become self-sufficient within a year, he firmly believes there is much more to life. He did not become a refugee to survive from day to day, but to *live*, to be fully alive. And he has a crystal-clear understanding of what this means for him: "Truly living means living in the hearts of people, not just doing your thing—everyone does that. I can't describe it very well, but what I'm trying to say is, if someone is glad you were born, because you help them, that's when you are truly alive."

Nabeel's vision propelled him to leave his country, but he came close to forgetting it when he was stuck in Sri Lanka. He says philosophically, "You realize it's not a fairy tale. Things don't work out because you want them to, or because you work hard. It just doesn't work that way. By the time you get a visa, you've lost the will to live; all you care about is just surviving again." This regression threatened the scope of Nabeel's sacrifice: "If you don't have that bigger will to live, some greater power that feeds your soul to go do something better, then it doesn't matter if you are living in that small area [in Quetta] or living here."

Nabeel has reclaimed his vision since being resettled and has no intention of losing it again. He fully intends to make others glad that he was born: "I want to work hard, to be in a position not just to help myself, but to help the people around me. What others did for me, I want to do for someone else."

19

"I HAVE A DREAM"

"MY DREAM IS COMING TRUE"

It is tempting to think that the only way refugees can realize their dreams is to manage to go to a wealthier place. Matthew from South Sudan defies this assumption. A refugee in Uganda, for the third time in his life, he looks every inch the happy man he says he is. This is because his dream is becoming reality. Matthew really wants to give South Sudanese teenagers in Uganda the lifeline of education, the same held out to him when he was a young refugee himself. He says, "When I was here as a child, I was helped, and from nowhere I became a teacher. I thank UNHCR [the United Nations High Commissioner for Refugees]. Now I am giving back what I have to my people."

Matthew lives in one of nineteen refugee settlements in the northern Adjumani District, a place evocative of the beauty of the Pearl of Africa, as Uganda is dubbed. During the hot season, the roads become dusty and water dries up. During the rainy season, the region turns green, giving one the feel of being on safari. It is here that Matthew felt compelled "to do something" when he returned to Uganda after fleeing a resurgence of violence in Juba, the capital of South Sudan, in 2016. He had spent eighteen years promoting education in his homeland as an antidote to war and what he saw in Uganda worried him: left to their own devices, refugee youth had acquired a reputation as idle troublemakers.

Like Ethiopia, Uganda has a commendable open-door policy, and it hosts the third-largest refugee population in the world, after Turkey and Pakistan, with more than 1.2 million refugees at the start of 2019. Most come from South Sudan and live in settlements in the north of the country. The district of Adjumani alone hosts more than two hundred thousand refugees. This is a big load for one of the world's poorest countries to shoulder, and essential services are seriously strained, not least education. Nearly half a million refugees in Uganda are children, less than eighteen years of age. Their enrollment rate in secondary school is only 14 percent. Even if they study hard, many cannot continue their education because there are not enough places in school, or because the fees are exorbitant for them, or for other reasons. Ugandan teenagers do not fare much better.

Matthew recalls, "When I came to Uganda this time, I said I have to do something for my people, instead of going back to South Sudan and roaming around. I sat down with some teachers and said, 'This is the next generation of South Sudan, so let us help them.'" When they asked how, Matthew's immediate answer was, "We should have a secondary school for them." The teachers were skeptical, but Matthew managed to get the green light from the UN and government agencies in record time. He started to organize afternoon classes in the primary school premises of the refugee settlement where he lives.

Less than three years later, the settlement is proud to have its own community secondary school, which is steadily growing in numbers and reputation. It hosts nearly one thousand students from both refugee and local communities, students who perform well in national certificate exams despite their difficult conditions and the limited resources. "I am happy because I see students are learning and my dream is coming true," says Matthew. The tempo of his happiness is regulated by the grades of his students in the national examinations and the expansion of his school.

By catering to Ugandan as well as refugee children, Matthew's school makes a great contribution to enhancing relationships between the two communities. "You know, even the local community is happy and praising me for what I've done," he says with a big smile. The settlements are situated alongside local villages and are very different from the typical images of a refugee camp that we might know from the news. Each refugee family is allocated a plot of land measuring thirty by thirty meters (approximately two-tenths of an acre). Only a trained eye can tell the difference between the houses of the two communities.

Refugees share services and natural resources with the host community. Coexistence is not always easy, however, and young people are blamed for many of the tensions and violent incidents.

Matthew is keen on education, not just as a way of keeping young refugees out of trouble, but because he believes wholeheartedly that it is the only way to stop the wars that have plagued his country for decades. He has had plenty of opportunity to observe the sorry state of South Sudan. Matthew's teaching career straddled the wars that first won the country its independence and later shattered it. In his work as a teacher, and later as an education advisor, Matthew traveled across South Sudan. He was dismayed by ethnic divisions so deep that the men of this or that tribal group did not dare to venture out of so-called POC (Protection of Civilians) sites, which had been set up by the UN.

Not the kind of person to shirk from monumental challenges, partly because he sees them as directly his own responsibility to address, Matthew wondered what he could do. "I asked myself, 'What should I do to create unity?' because the situation is really very bad and if such a thing continues, South Sudan will not have peace." Matthew pinned his hopes on education: "My biggest hope is that in ten years South Sudan will not be the same, because we are trying to transform the mind-set of people, so they look at each other as brothers and sisters." Back in South Sudan, Matthew worked indefatigably toward this end and now, in Uganda, he is doing the same.

Matthew's other reason for backing education is that he wants to give young people born and bred in a culture of war a feasible alternative to fighting. He wants to give them knowledge and skills, "so that they will be able to do something and not look at a gun as the only option." Matthew has intimately experienced the merciless horror of South Sudan's wars. Actually, he was born in Uganda, when his parents lived there as refugees in the 1970s. He says, "I was taken back to South Sudan when there was relative peace, and I completed my primary school and started my secondary. Again, in 1989, we were chased away and came to Uganda as refugees, where I continued with my studies." The way Matthew tells his story, the life-changing events of exile and return are punctuated by the precise memory of where and when he went to school. That is what takes precedence above everything else.

Matthew was nineteen when his family was chased out of the town of Nimule at the border of Uganda in 1989. South Sudan was not yet independent then, though it was fighting to become so, and rebels from the Sudan People's Liberation Army (SPLA) had overrun the town. "You know, the problem we have in South Sudan is they don't *spare*." Matthew emphasizes this last word heavily and elaborates: "Like, if their target was only taking the town from the government, then they should have spared the civilians after taking the town. In our case, they don't do that. They say, 'You have been collaborating with the enemy. You are also the enemy.' This is what had been happening." On the day the SPLA appeared, Matthew and his family fled together with the other residents of Nimule to cross to Uganda via the Nile River. They jumped into canoes amid a hail of bullets. Matthew's family reached the other side of the river safely and lived as refugees for nine years, during which time Matthew became a teacher.

He returned to South Sudan in 1998 and stayed until 2016, when "we were chased away again." This time, South Sudan was already independent, and its president, Salva Kiir, and vice president, Riek Machar, had locked horns in a power struggle that devastated their country. Matthew was in the wrong place at the wrong time—the capital, when Machar turned up with one thousand heavily armed bodyguards, provoking renewed violence. Matthew left Juba: "There was no way; I had to leave. I left all my belongings there, even my computer, everything." He went first to his hometown but then, he says, "I saw people running away too." So Matthew came to Uganda with his wife and children.

Matthew is in Uganda to stay for now, because he wants to see the long-term results of the work he has started, not only in high academic scores, although those make him very happy, but in young people who will return to South Sudan as citizens, and not just as Dinka, Nuer, or one of the scores of other tribes that make up this divided nation.

"I HOPE FOR A BETTER LIFE"

Martin has a vision that keeps him going too. It comes across more as a compulsion, and a poignant one at that. Since he was forced to become a child soldier in South Sudan and to kill a man, Martin is determined to spend the rest of his life making up for what he has done and, if he can, "to repay the people I once hurt."

He says, "I want to be a great person in my life because I've killed now. I want to be a successful man, so I can repay. I will give out all I have to the poor so that I can please my God." Martin has a plan for how to go about this: "I hope one day I will be a lawyer. I can speak for the lonely and always protect the poor. That way I will repay what I have done." Becoming a lawyer has always been Martin's dream. "My dad said he would sacrifice everything to make sure I became the lawyer I asked for," he says. Martin will most likely have to manage without his father's help now. He whispers, "But now, I don't know if my father is alive or dead. I don't know."

As soon as Martin reached Uganda after running away from South Sudan, he moved around the refugee settlements, trying to find his father and siblings, to no avail. He has not given up: "I hope I still have my brother and my sister; I want to see them again." Martin was loathe to stay in the settlements, describing them as "weird." In a thread of silver lining to the cloud that engulfed his life, he found a place to call home. It was his first port of call when he arrived in Uganda, the only house he knew, because his father used to rent it when Martin came to school in Adjumani, in happier times. Martin knew the landlady, a widow called Mary, and asked her if she could give him a home. "Mary got scared when she saw me, but she let me in. I explained everything to her and she accepted me," he recalls. "She treats me quite well because she understands me better than any other person and she used to be friendly with my family."

Martin has tried his best to get by but faces enormous obstacles. Everything in his life is precarious. He managed to get into a school in Kampala, the capital of Uganda. Mary helped him with the fees, and he worked hard between terms, doing all sorts of odd jobs. But then they fell on hard times. "Mary was operated, and she's down; she needs the money for herself," explains Martin briefly. "Last year I almost dropped out from school because she couldn't pay for me anymore. If she eats, I eat. If she doesn't, I don't. That is when there is no food in the house. I ate three meals in my father's house but now I take only once." Another fear is that Mary will be evicted from "her small piece of land" because of him. It appears that Mary's family members do not trust Martin, perhaps because they know or intuit something about his past. He is very worried about this misperception. "They say one day their sister will be killed because of me," he frets. "They say one day something will come over me and I will kill."

It seems they are not the only ones to say things in this vein: "My age mates, sometimes they tell me, 'You will kill us.' They tell me I am a killer." When I ask why they say such things, Martin replies, "I feel they know my story. Sometimes they mock at me." Silence follows this disclosure. Regardless of why he is labeled a killer, Martin gets hugely upset about it, because it is a reminder of the moment he wants so much to erase. "The memory of killing that man comes to me, even in class. It tortures my mind." Martin falls silent again and then continues, "I just want to rub off everything. I want to rub off being called a killer. I want to be a different person."

Martin describes the remorse that stalks him as a "bad feeling all over me," even when he tries to "fix a false appearance to make me look good." There is the persistent belief that his unhappiness could be a result of bad karma: "Maybe the reason why I am suffering is because I killed that man. He may have a family somewhere and they may be suffering because I killed him."

Martin is suffering enormously not only because of the life he was forced to take, but also because of the life that was snatched away from him. He says, "I feel jealous when I see people seated with their family; they are happy. I once had a very happy family and now all I've got . . ." Another sentence destined to taper off into nothing. After a few minutes, Martin says, "I want to bring another happy family again." He wipes away his tears furiously and says with resolve, "And I will."

There is one person Martin remembers and blames for the destruction of his family. He describes him as "the man who betrayed us, who called us from the house, and caused my mother's death." Martin saw this man in Uganda, in one of the refugee settlements. He says, "I know his face and I have seen him here. I wanted to go straight to him but my friend stopped me. I let him go." The look in Martin's eyes and the tone of his voice are implacable when he mentions this man: "He is still alive. Because of him, I lost my family. I am all alone."

With northern Uganda too close for comfort to South Sudan, Martin needs more distance if he is ever to move on. He feels this keenly: "I don't want to stay even here. I want to find my way somewhere. I want to go far away and leave this place of chaos. I want to meet new people in my life to be my brothers, kindhearted people like Mary." Martin has made another good friend since coming to Uganda, a man named Samuel who is a bit older than he is. Their first encounter took place in South Sudan and did not bode well for friendship. The two set eyes on each other when Martin was standing by the roadside to flag down vehicles so his captors could rob them, another nefarious deed he was forced to commit. Samuel was one of the victims. When Samuel saw Martin again in Uganda, he instantly recognized Martin's face and voice. "He attacked me to beat me but, after understanding about me, he became my friend, the only good friend I have here," Martin says.

After listening to Martin for hours, the impression I take away is that his spirit, all but crushed out of him, survives. He harbors hope stronger than his shame and is fighting his demons with every ounce of strength he has. And he has faith. Toward the end of our conversation, he says, "I always pray when I sleep. All my hope is in God. I know everything happens because of him. One day he shall give me the face of happiness."

When I ask him if there is anything else he wants to share, Martin ends on a note of encouragement, for himself and for others: "I'd like to tell any other refugees like me, sometimes we have weird feelings, but being a refugee is not the end of life. I hope for a better life. I know everything can change for me and we can change the entire South Sudan to become a peaceful place. I still have a lot of brothers, a lot of friends who could never manage to run away, but still we hope for peace and God's blessings." Amen.

20

REJECTION AND HOSPITALITY IN EUROPE

AN ECSTATIC REUNION . . . AND THEN WHAT?

Emil could not believe his eyes. But it was true enough: there was his mother smiling at him from a photo stored on a friend's phone. Emil had given up his family for lost after they were separated on Libyan shores while trying to board a boat for Europe. The teenager had eventually managed to make the journey alone and was in a camp in Genoa, in northern Italy, mulling his next move. Since Emil did not have a phone, he asked to borrow his friend's. Imagine his delighted incredulity when he saw the photo of his mother. Emil immediately asked his friend, "Do you know this woman?" His friend replied, "Yes, she arrived with my older brother, but I don't know where she is now."

He explained that his brother had taken a group photo of those who had traveled on the boat with him to Italy. Considering that more than 181,000 people crossed from North Africa to Italy in 2016, the year Emil's mother crossed, it is quite incredible that Emil found himself next to the brother of someone who traveled with her. Emil pressed his friend: "Where did this lady go? Do you know?"

When contacted, the brother did not have any news of Emil's mother, save that she was pregnant when they met, but he asked around and learned that perhaps she had gone to France. The precious snippet of information convinced Emil: "When I heard the word 'France,' I said, 'I must go there too; perhaps I will find my mother.' I understood nothing else, just that I had to find her." Emil walked from Genoa to Milan, and then onward to Ventimiglia, the last Italian town before the French border and a destination of refugees hoping to cross from Italy to France.

Emil knows how to tell a story: there are no extraneous details, only the unembellished facts the listener needs to know to follow his journey and the reasoning behind it. "When I reached Ventimiglia, I just took the train, and they caught me at the border," he continues. "I explained my story, but the police did not allow me to enter just like that, and they turned me back." Back in Italy, an elderly French man approached Emil and asked him why he was so sad and alone. "He asked me in French why I was there, and did I have a problem to pay my ticket. I explained that I was looking for my mother, that she was in France, but I didn't know where." The elderly man paid Emil's train ticket to Marseille, a few hours' ride away. In a second stroke of luck, Emil was not apprehended at the border this time and managed to reach his destination without any identification papers.

Entering France was one small victory, but Emil still had no idea where or how to look for his parents. "I spent two months without knowing what to do because it is not like Africa here," he says. Emil found a place in a squat and spent six months searching here and there as best he knew how. Meanwhile, a man named Matthieu was also trying to find Emil's mother through the official asylum agency in Marseille. Matthieu worked for a local NGO and had befriended Emil. They tracked down not only Emil's mother but the rest of his family too. To surprise Emil, Matthieu found some excuse to send him to the address where his family was living. "Ahhhh, I went mad with joy," Emil says. "I found my father too—he had come here—and found my mother. Everyone was there."

Their ecstatic reunion was the stuff of dreams, but Emil's family is not yet secure. "It hasn't been easy," says Emil. "We applied for asylum; we are at the beginning of the process. We did the interview and are waiting for an answer. I really want to live in Paris and to do something with my life." But they do not know whether France will accept their application for asylum. Until they get their answer, Emil's family will be on edge: "We are always worried. I truly hope France accepts us and we will not stay like this."

This gnawing uncertainty is the fate of every person who knocks at the door of a country that is not his own to seek asylum. The sheer relief of having made it to a safe place, usually after a harrowing journey, is superseded by anxiety and frustration when things do not swiftly fall into place as hoped. Sometimes, those seeking asylum realize that they might not be so safe after all, because they find themselves up against overstretched and off-putting systems that are increasingly dictated by a culture of rejection and disbelief. The outlook for Emil's family is chancy: in 2018, France rejected nearly three-quarters of asylum applications from Guineans. One possible outcome is that his little sister will be granted asylum because she risks FGM if returned to Guinea. The rest of her family could receive permission to stay until she reaches adulthood.

Amadou, also from Guinea, is understandably worried about his chances of finding asylum in France, where he went via Italy after leaving the torments of Libya behind. He is finding life "very, very difficult" contrary to expectations that "when I arrived here, perhaps my suffering would be over." At least he has a place to live now, renting a bed in the apartment of a friend. He recalls, "When I got here, I didn't know a soul. It was winter and I slept outside in the park. The worst thing was the rain. Finding food was not difficult because if you ask people in the street for a euro, they give you, and you buy a slice of pizza and a drink." France grapples with a pressing shortage of accommodations for people who come to seek asylum, which they are doing in increasing numbers. In 2018, France ranked second only to Germany in the EU in terms of numbers of asylum applicants. More than half were not given a place to stay, and so their only choice was to find a night shelter or to stay on the streets, as Amadou did.

Amadou has been in France for one year when I see him at the parish house, where he is learning how to write and to converse in French. "I can manage with French although I only went to school for three years, until my father died, and then we could no longer afford it," he says. The volunteers who organize the language classes try to create a friendly space by preparing and sharing a meal with their students. Amadou looks and feels at home there, just like any other young man, and it is sad to watch the cheerful façade give way to agitation when he talks about the nightmare of Libya and the nagging worry of what will become of him in France.

Amadou has suffered a setback in his asylum application. He is one of thousands of "Dubliners" in Europe, a quaint term for refugees who face return to the EU state where their fingerprints first showed up, per the Dublin Regulation. Although return is relatively rare, the process means several months longer in limbo. "At the prefecture, they gave me a flight ticket to return to Italy," says Amadou. "But I'm not going back to Italy; I want to stay here. I don't understand why Italy." No wonder refugees are frustrated with the policies that govern their lives and their futures: the policies not only seem arbitrary, but also are confusing.

"WE ARE LUCKY TO WELCOME HIM"

In a miniature chateau nestled in the heart of a historic village in Aix-en-Provence, southern France, Abdul sits in a room that enticingly blends comfort with splendor. The room has high windows set in thick walls of stone, and a fire crackles in the magnificent hearth, surrounded by homey sofas and antique furniture. Abdul is a man in his mid-twenties from Guinea, and he is the guest of Marcel and Jeanne, an elderly French couple who are hosts with the Welcome Network. This national network links volunteer families and religious congregations to asylum seekers who need a place to stay for a while.

But Abdul is unable to make the most of the hospitality extended to him. Jeanne confesses to Raphael, who works for Welcome in Marseille and who accompanies me on the visit, that she is worried about her guest. Abdul is depressed and eating very little, and his medication has not made any discernible difference as yet. Abdul's appearance justifies her concern. He offers answers to the questions put to him in a mechanical and dull voice and looks away. Abdul is obsessing over the idea that he might be returned to Guinea, and this fear gives him no rest: "I have worries in my head and sadness in my heart. Will they accept my story or not?"

Abdul came to France via Italy, managing to cross at Ventimiglia because he was sitting in the front of the train while border guards checked the back. Raphael reassures Abdul that things will work out somehow. They discuss where he is in the asylum process while Jeanne tries to make sense of it, too, asking about this or that official slip of paper mailed to Abdul. She also wants to know more about the situation in Guinea. Their palpable concern warms the room as much as the fire does. There is nothing cloying or condescending about their desire to help.

Abdul is reciprocating the hospitality as best he can, by pitching in on the household chores. He offers to help Marcel rake leaves in the garden and cooks a meal of rice and fish for his hosts. In the longest speech that he volunteers, unprompted, Abdul says, "They have welcomed me as part of their family; they treat me like their son. So I cannot stay here without doing anything. I wanted to do something for them."

Jeanne dispatches her husband to buy three sweet potatoes for Abdul's lunch because she knows he likes them. Hearing her instructions, Abdul smiles for the first time. As we take our leave, we meet Marcel returning from his errand, and he waves the potatoes at us cheerfully. That image stays with me, of hospitality that listens to and becomes part of the story of one refugee. Marcel and Jeanne are doing this because of a firm belief in universal fraternity that is sorely tried by the reluctance of wealthy countries to welcome people in need from poorer parts of the world. Marcel spoke in French throughout the interview, but there was one thing he said in halting English, to make sure I got the message: "We are lucky to help him, to welcome him."

A MORALIZING APPROACH BASED ON CONVENIENT CLASSIFICATION

European governments do not appear to subscribe to this point of view. Rather, their decisions reveal a ruthless intent to set boundaries to this spirit of hospitality. Witness the huge investment in external border controls, to stop people from coming in the first place; the browbeating of NGO vessels that bring rescued people to Europe's shores; and the pushbacks by border guards. As for those people who still manage to breach the walls of Fortress Europe, the system takes a moralizing approach, implying that protection should be saved for those who are "genuine" and who "deserve" it, and not for "fake" refugees, who arrive here without a valid claim on our compassion.

The system tends toward facile formulae to decide whether an asylum claim is valid or not. One's country of origin is either "safe" (at least

in parts) or "unsafe." One is either a "refugee" or an "economic migrant," with the latter all but demonized for having the temerity to turn
up. French president Emmanuel Macron is one of several political
leaders to play on this rigid distinction, saying his country would welcome the first but exclude the second, a category he classified as "those
that don't belong."

Arbitrary categorizations, parroted with lazy ease, threaten to deflect
attention from each person's unique story and need for protection. Reality does not fit neatly into convenient classifications, especially the
reality of violent, repressive, and impoverished countries, with rule of
law compromised to varying degrees. It is frequently impossible to draw
a line between "economic" and "life threatening" in the reasons given
by an individual for deciding to leave such places.

In 2018, the fate of 891,000 asylum applicants was decided across
the EU, and over one-third received some kind of protection. The
overall number of decisions included 309,000 appeals, of which nearly
40 percent were accepted, *after being turned down the first time.* A
successful outcome has as much to do with how applicants tell their
story as how it is heard and judged. One telling fact is that applicants
coming from the same country can get very different results across the
EU, depending on the country where they apply. Just consider the wide
span of recognition rates of Afghan asylum claims in 2016, which
ranged between 2.5 and 97 percent. There are Afghans who live for
years in one country, learn the language, and find a job, only to be
shown the door when their application for asylum is refused and their
options run out. Some go from one European country to another to find
a place that will accept them.

One such man is Abdullah, to whom I am introduced during a language class for refugees. The location is Rome, and the students are
learning Italian, but the volunteers are just like those in Marseille, in
terms of both friendliness and individualized creative teaching. Abdullah spent years in Sweden, which turned down his asylum application
three times and threatened him with deportation. When he overstayed,
his clandestine life literally made Abdullah sick. "I lost time there.
Sometimes I worked, sometimes not. I had no document; I lived 'black'
for three years," he says. "I couldn't speak to people. I was afraid,
maybe they will tell the police and deport me. Living alone was too
much depression. I went to a psychologist and he gave me medicine. I

knew that if I stayed there, I would die." Abdullah left and applied for asylum in Italy, where he was accepted as a refugee, getting the chance to restart his life.

Then there is Masood, an Afghan driver who attends the language classes in Marseille. He lived in Finland for two years before being shown the door. "They did not give me papers; I don't why," he says. Masood is hoping that France will give him a more sympathetic hearing. Meanwhile, time cannot pass fast enough. Masood has not seen his family in six years and is terribly lonely. "You want to know my story?" he asks. "Here it is: I go to the beach and I sit there, thinking of my kids, how to send money to feed and to clothe them, always I think like this. I have four: the eldest is fourteen and the youngest is five." Masood never even saw his youngest child because he fled Afghanistan just before the boy was born. When Masood left, he never imagined it would take him so long to find a safe place, and to bring his family to join him. Until he can see them again, Masood lives for those times when he can talk to his family on the phone.

ANOTHER CHANCE AT LIFE

Pitting the individual stories of refugees against the policies that decide their fate quickly reveals the gap between the two and the frequent inhumanity of the latter. Tigiste was rejected the first time she applied for asylum in France. Her story was met with disbelief. Then she was granted refugee status on appeal.

Tigiste is lucky because she has received tremendous support from the Welcome Network and has lived with several host families. It is at the home of one such family that I meet her. She has her own granny flat on the grounds of their spacious home and is much loved. She muses, "This is a new experience in my life. I didn't know them, they didn't know me, but I believe one thing: if you give on the table good thing, you find better than good thing." At first, it was difficult for Tigiste to accept she was safe and loved. After being harmed so much, she was literally moved to tears by the care she received. She tries to convey what she means: "The first family I stayed with, I cried all night because I have seen too many devil people in my life, in Eritrea, Sudan, ibya. Sometimes, I see good-hearted people, so I cry. Perhaps God helped me to survive to come back here so I can see this."

While Tigiste gradually settled down in France, the uppermost concern on her mind was to locate Ermias. "I needed to search for my baby because he is the only thing I have. I have no family, but now I see him as a second life of mine, and a gift of God." Tigiste used all her contacts and ingenuity to find Mrs. Getachew, who had taken Ermias with her safely from Libya to Ethiopia. Tigiste was finally rewarded when one of her friends tracked down the brother of her son's guardian. "I wrote to this man, and then I called, and it was her brother! I ran and I told everyone, 'I found my baby!'" Tigiste got in touch with Mrs. Getachew and learned that Ermias, now a toddler, was faring well in Addis Ababa. "She was very happy to hear from me. She thought I was dead," says Tigiste, beaming. "She sent me photos and now I speak with my son. He is my blessing." Ermias knows that Tigiste is his mother and is waiting to join her in France. There are still bureaucratic hurdles to overcome, but Tigiste lives in hope.

Tigiste badly needs someone to call her own. She has pinned her hopes for a new beginning on her son: "I thank God because perhaps I will forget everything that happened in my life now that he gave me a baby." After she was already in France, Tigiste heard news about her father that broke her heart. "I met a guy from Eritrea. When I asked him if he knew my father, he cried and told me everything," she says, tears springing to her eyes again. "Everyone knew my father, because he was a good pastor, and this man I met was in prison in Eritrea. The government told my father, 'You need to change your religion,' and he refused, so they shot and killed him."

Today, Tigiste admits to a keen sense of isolation, even with loving friends to host her. "I am lonely," she says frankly. "If you have brothers and sisters, maybe you share something, or if you have father, mother. I don't know what love of family is. I forget, because I have been living lonely a long time." Apart from the loneliness, Tigiste is still struggling to come to terms with her past. The persistent playback of memories distresses her to this day: "It's not easy, especially at night. When I close my eyes, I see everything." Tigiste has already come a long way. But she knows that some things, much as she would like to leave them behind, are with her to stay. "I've seen too many psychologists but I can't forget. This is my life; I can't forget it, even if I want to."

Outwardly, Tigiste looks fine, as do most of the other refugees I meet in the European cities where they are trying to start over. However, close to the surface, many harbor anguish and anxiety, disappointed hope, and so many unanswered "what if" questions. Getting protection is a huge step in the right direction, but even that is not enough to sweep all the negatives away.

"GOD ALWAYS HELPS"

"Papa, all the other children in class have fathers and mothers with cars, but I must take the bus. Why you don't have a car?" The innocent question of Anwar's eight-year-old son hurts, every time. "My son doesn't understand that his father is here with nothing," he says sadly. "In Pakistan, I had everything; here, no, but the kids don't understand."

Anwar left Pakistan when his dreams literally went up in smoke. The Taliban set fire to his school because he welcomed Christian and Muslim children to study together. Then they tried to kill him, but his best friend got in the way of the bullets and died instead. Anwar escaped from the country where he had everything except safety, and paid eight thousand euros to go to Europe, where he has almost nothing except safety.

"When I paid, the smuggler told me it was easy to get a document. But it was not easy at all," says Anwar. He traveled for forty-five days through Iran, Turkey, and Greece before reaching his destination, exhausted and petrified in body, mind, and spirit. "In those days, half of my mind was numb. My four little children were in Pakistan, I was going I didn't know where, and I didn't know if I would live or die, you understand?" He remembers how one person fell as they were walking by night through the mountains between Iran and Pakistan: "We never saw him again."

Anwar asked for asylum, which was granted. It was only after five years that he managed to get his family to join him. "When they came, I saw my children had grown so much," he says, scrolling through the photos on his phone to find one of his family the day they arrived. A big smile replaces the perpetually hassled expression on his face when he shows it to me.

Anwar and his family live in a picturesque town, which he asks me not to name to protect his anonymity. He reels off the list of costs he must pay each month with a salary of seven hundred euros for working double shifts as a carer in a home for the elderly—so much for apartment rent, so much for utility bills, so much for food, schoolbooks, and other family expenses. Anwar can barely make ends meet. He admits to finding life "so difficult" but says that "God is great and he helps." This is Anwar's motto, and it is what he reminds his son when the car question comes up: "I tell him, 'God always helps. Be calm.'"

Still, it is not easy for Anwar to stomach the difference between now and then. "In Pakistan, I had my own house, cows, horses, fields with mango and orange trees, but here . . ." He stops midsentence and looks down at his hands with reddening eyes. Then he says in a low voice, "Eh, *si*." There is nothing more to say.

21

"YOU NEED TO LISTEN TO THAT VOICE"

THE POWER OF A SINGLE GESTURE

"**I** have the feeling that Catania is my place, my city, and that I have known it all my life." Abdel Mohammed, who remembers so clearly the day he jumped into a boat to get away from Libya's civil war, came to Sicily and stayed. He has been living in Catania for eight years and works as a cultural mediator. Echoing Nabeel in San Diego, he says, "Today, I feel fortunate. I feel I can help others too. I can share with people what I have." This is what Abdel wants to do most of all, to be close to and help those "who are in more difficult situations than I am."

In 2015, when the number of refugees seeking asylum in Europe rose sharply, Abdel made good his intentions. Together with Lucien, a refugee from Ivory Coast, Abdel started to go out on the streets to see what they could do to help. "When the big wave of people came, many were sleeping on the streets. We searched for medicines, food, and clothes. I have many friends from Catania who helped, like one who bought twenty-eight bus tickets for some to keep traveling." Even after the moment of crisis passed, the two refugees continued to go out on the streets once a week. Abdel explains, "We dedicate this day to the homeless. We accompany them and help them find a place to sleep, to work. They can call us anytime."

Abdel's motivation stems from the desire to multiply the joy he felt when someone helped him. It was a Sudanese man in Libya named Sheikh who was there for Abdel when he was badly in need. This was way back, on Abdel's very first day in Libya, after two weeks crossing the desert. He was tired, thirsty, hungry, and penniless. "I was in the middle of the city where I knew no one. I was there for hours, staring at people, but no one stopped." Then Abdel saw a man putting something in his car and decided to try his luck. "I told him I had crossed the Sahara and needed a place to stay for the night. He could see I was shaking. He took me to the market and bought me clothes and then took me to his house."

At Sheikh's house, there was a group of Sudanese boys, and each one brought Abdel some of their own clothes. Every day they gave him money to make do, and within a week they had found him work in a poultry farm and shop. The timely support was all Abdel needed to regain his footing. He prospered and eventually started to manage the farm himself. In the three years he stayed in Libya, the home of Sheikh was his home, even after he moved out to live alone. "Every Friday I used to go back. They were my friends, my family."

The hospitality of Sheikh left a lasting impact on Abdel. "Precisely at that moment, I understood very well what I wanted to do and how I wanted to live my life. It is like this moment became a point of reference for me, for everything I do." However, even after sleepless nights spent looking after homeless refugees on the streets of Catania, Abdel says he can never do enough. "Everything I do, I feel like it is nothing compared to when these people helped me."

The force of Abdel's feeling bears witness to just how meaningful a simple gesture can be. The bigger the need, the deeper the significance of the gesture that tries to meet it. Abdel says, "I was so lost in the city and I chose this man, I don't know why. When he said, 'Wait two minutes,' I was so happy, because he was telling me, 'Wait, you will come with me.' Anytime I do something, I see how such gestures can change people's lives."

There is one more important lesson that Sheikh and his home community of Sudanese youth taught Abdel: to be open to help everyone, not only those who are like you, who come from your own group: "I don't have the sense of belonging to a particular group. I don't say I lost it, but I have opened up more towards the other. You rarely find me with Eritreans; you find me with the whole world."

"WE CAN DO MORE THAN THEY THINK"

Armed with these and more insights that come naturally to his philo-sophical self, Abdel is busy propagating them in Catania. He has co-founded an association called Africa Unita with Lucien. When we meet, the two of them are full of pride over a big event that Africa Unita has just organized with the International Fellowship of Reconciliation. The international organization reached out to the local association and to-gether they held two days of encounters in Catania. One highlight was a supper in the town mosque for more than 120 people, including many homeless migrants. Abdel explains, "We created this moment for those living in difficult times and for delegates from around the world. We wanted to say, 'This is the problem, be aware,' and we opened the mosque to create a moment of encounter and understanding."

Lucien wanted to set up the association "to show that refugees and migrants can do more than people think," and to create a space for all those of goodwill to do something together. "There are people who want to help but don't know how, so we let them know we need them by our side and vice versa," he says. The international event was impor-tant in his eyes because "we had the opportunity to speak, because usually the Catania authorities meet to speak among themselves about our problems." Lucien chuckles and continues, "So we said, 'You need to listen to what we have to say.'"

Although Lucien and Abdel are happily settled in Catania, they can-not imagine living there forever. "I want to go back home. This is one of the things I want most," Abdel says more than once. Lucien is making serious plans to open a primary school in Divo, a city in southern Ivory Coast. He has a very clear message for the children he hopes to teach someday: "We want to let them know that they can make a life for themselves there and that life overseas is perhaps not what they think." He intends to create a space where returned migrants can share the details of their lives abroad to open the eyes of their young compatriots who are tempted to go to Europe to find work.

Lucien left Ivory Coast because his political activism put him in mortal danger. In other words, he had no choice. However, he works with unaccompanied minors and has listened to many stories of those who could and would have returned home were it not for a crushing sense of failure and humiliation. They went away from their country to seek a better life, but what they found was worse than what they left behind. "Some want to return but they are ashamed to start from zero," Lucien says. "They sell everything to pay their travel. One of the worst things is that when they arrive in Libya, they are kidnapped, and their family must sell everything to pay their ransom. So, if you return, what will you do? You won't have any respect."

Lucien believes in the power of telling stories, not only to fellow Africans, but also to others who do not know or understand what people like him go through. He says, "Some people don't even believe such stories exist, but refugees and migrants carry the scars, and they will never forget." Abdel shares his friend's conviction: "I feel we have to speak out. Otherwise people will continue to have the same idea about us, the idea they imagine, not the truth, and if you don't change that idea, it will stay."

Over the past twenty years, whenever I have approached refugees with a request to share their story, most have jumped at the chance. All over the world, there are sweeping stereotypes about refugees: about who they are, why they turn up, and the risks they supposedly pose to life as we know it. The stereotypes miss or distort most of what it is truly important to know. This is why refugees want to set the record straight by telling their own stories, not to have someone else label and pre-judge them and get it completely and utterly wrong. Refugees do it for themselves, for their own sense of self and dignity, but also out of solidarity with others who will become refugees, because they need and deserve to be understood.

"REFUGEES ARE NOT WHAT YOU THINK THEM"

"I wouldn't leave my country if I were not desperate. I had my life and I had everything. But I didn't feel safe anymore. I was about to lose my life. You need to hear that; you need to listen to that voice."

Waleed feels he has a personal responsibility to get this message across on behalf of all refugees. He eagerly agrees to talk to me because he hopes this book will spread the word. We sit in his office in San Diego. Waleed was resettled to the United States in 2009 and is thankful for the opportunity he received, for himself and especially for his two sons. But this affable man wants Americans to know why he needed to migrate in the first place. He says, "I wish people could hear why we want to come here. I wish they understand the need—it's not because we want to go on vacation, it's not because we want to live the dream, or to have better Internet. It's because we are afraid. You know, I fled for my life and for my family's life. People need to hear that."

The moment Waleed realized he was going to have to quit his homeland came when his name appeared on a terrorist hit list. Waleed is Iraqi. In his country, he worked for years for the UN to implement community mobilization programs before being headhunted by the US Army and accepting work with them. "And then, all of a sudden, I am on the target list. I still remember that day. It was curfew time and I heard a knock at my door at about 8:00 p.m. I was thinking, 'Who's going to knock at my door now?' I opened and there was the guy who used to drive me around the projects. He was, like, 'Some people I know saw your name in a list in a mosque and you're next.'"

Waleed needed no further explanation. He was familiar with what the list meant: insurgent groups in Iraq posted the names of their intended targets, picked because they worked for the Americans. He recalls, "I had a mix of feelings: 'I'm going to challenge them. They're going to kill me. I'm going to escape.' My family, my kids . . . a lot of things." After a sleepless night, Waleed crept out of his house in the city of Mosul, dived into his car, and sped to Kirkuk, a city in northern Iraq that was considered safe. But Waleed would never feel safe in his homeland again. When insurgents kidnapped (and later released) his brother, that was it. Waleed applied for resettlement to the United States and arrived with his family and eight big pieces of luggage. He laughs as he supplies this detail: "We were four, so two each."

Ten years later, the biggest boon for Waleed is that he can sleep peacefully at night. For most of us, this is a cliché, but not for him. "When you go to bed here, you set your head on the pillow, and the only thing you think is, 'I have a job to do tomorrow,' or 'I'm going on vacation,' or whatever. Back home, you think, 'Am I going to come back from work tomorrow?' You never know. Maybe a suicide bomber will hug you or something."

Waleed's family is well settled. He has a good job, and he grins when he talks about his two sons, who are "very Americanized. Like sponges, they soak everything up." One is already at university and the other, age fifteen, is in high school. But starting "from zero" was not easy, neither for him nor for countless refugees he met when he worked for a resettlement agency. And yet, Waleed says, "Refugees are very dedicated, hard workers. They have the passion to start a new life. I would give every positive word to describe them."

Waleed feels that he needs to highlight refugees' virtues because of what he perceives as the "stigma" surrounding them, "like, refugees are taking advantage of social security services, they are on welfare. Yes, some of them are, and so was I for the first couple of months when I arrived. But then I started contributing to the American economy. My family is doing so, and my friends are doing so, so refugees are not what you think them." Do such comments come to his ears frequently, I ask, about refugees being stereotyped as spongers? "From people, oh yes, I've heard this," he says.

Nabeel from Pakistan, who is ecstatically happy to be in the United States, also feels an aura of difference surrounding him sometimes. He discerns it in the way some people react to him when they learn he is a refugee. "I work at a hotel front desk and we have people coming from all around US. There are people who get shocked when I tell them I am a refugee," he says with a smile. "You can see it on their face: 'Oh, he's a refugee, and he's working at the front desk.'" Others are surprised he can speak English.

Nabeel puts this attitude of wonder down not to hostility, but to ignorance. Tentatively he suggests that it's about labels: "I think the words 'refugee' and 'migrant' aren't looked at in the right way, as they're supposed to be. When you use these words, they look at you differently. It's not the people; it's how these words are painted. They've heard the big picture of how too many refugees destroy our country but they haven't seen anyone up close."

Nabeel has a message for people "who have those images painted of a refugee or migrant," and it is quite simply to go from the big picture, which is often misleading, to the small ones. "Everyone has a story. Before judging someone, just try to understand their story—ask them where they are from, what made them who they are and why. That story makes us, us, today." He echoes the message that Waleed is fervently promoting: "The people who are unfortunately refugees, they don't decide to be refugees. No one wants to leave home but life forces you. And if everyone tries to understand a refugee's story, I think they'd have a much better perspective."

Nabeel has seen this for himself: "When you start talking to people, about where you come from, what's your story, that's when they smile and be happy. I feel like they feel proud of their country because it's doing something to help refugees."

22

A QUESTION OF BELONGING

"I FEEL I DON'T BELONG HERE"

Refugees who net the golden opportunity of resettlement have made it. Right? Their story has a happy ending. They can now realistically start over. There is some truth in this. The refugees whom I meet in San Diego are lyrical in their praises of the NGO charged with helping them to settle in the United States, to fill in the forms, to learn English, to discover how to get around, to get a job, and so on. They need all the help they can get: refugees who resettle in the United States must hit the ground running to keep up with the swift pace of life and to become self-sufficient as quickly as possible.

When I go to the Promised Land, the way I can best describe what I observe among the refugees is a bittersweet appreciation of what was gained and what was lost. Both limitless quantities are constantly weighed in the balance of their lives. Waleed says, "My life got harder here because I was so comfortable back there, but when I see my kids, it's rewarding. At least they are in a safe place. I see how they are growing, I see the opportunities, and how different life is here compared to there. When I feel I might have made a bad decision to move to the US, right away, I think of my nieces and nephews in Iraq and how hard their life is compared to my kids' life."

Waleed ticks off all the material ways in which his family is better off now: education, health, technology, and future prospects. Then, in the same breath, he adds, "Home is home. I was born and raised there. All my memories are there. Everything is there." This is a refrain, especially among older refugees, who miss their land, their homes, and their families terribly. Waleed continues, "It's been ten years and I feel I don't belong here; I feel that especially since my whole family is still there. I miss home, yeah. My mum, my brothers, my sisters, we are very family oriented. We live our lives together. I call my brother almost every day. Just, 'What's going on?' We are very connected."

THIS IS ME

Fatima, an attractive Iraqi woman in her late twenties, starts off in an upbeat tone, telling me how she considers herself to be very lucky with "two beautiful kids and a good job," not to mention wonderful American friends. "They really adopted me," she says of her friends. "If you don't have someone to support you here, life is very hard, especially for those who don't have work experience in the US. I am so happy and thankful for everything I have." Fatima is especially grateful for the help she received when newly arrived and pregnant. "I had a hard pregnancy: preeclampsia, blood pressure, diabetes. I didn't have a car, I didn't know how to use public transportation, and my friend used to take me for the doctor's appointment at hospital."

Four years down the line, Fatima has a job with a resettlement agency. She loves her work because it entails helping newly arrived refugees. "We really take care of them—help them to find an apartment, to apply for benefits, to buy furniture, to enroll their kids in school." She likes the airport pickups best: "It's great, welcoming people. They live the same experience I went through, so it is like a circle of life: someone helped me when I came here and now it is my turn to pay back."

I ask Fatima about her own early days in the United States. Her voice wobbles unexpectedly when she replies. "I didn't want to come," she says. "I didn't want to leave my family: my parents, my sisters, and my brothers. They are all there. But because of all that is going on there, everyone was saying, 'Yes, you should go. You'll have a different life there,' you know, the American dream or something." Fatima has accepted that she will never stop pining for home, and she is endlessly sorry that her family is missing out on precious moments in her life, "like birthday parties. Every year my kids they are getting bigger."

Fatima presents a confident and impeccable front. She admits, laughing, that it takes daily effort to look good and to get her three kids ready at the same time. Skillfully applied makeup highlights her natural beauty, and the style and colors of her outfit fit her perfectly. However, a glimmer of disquiet is discernible in the flood of her words. Her English is excellent but she mentions an accent she is trying to get rid of. "I am working on it but I don't think it will go away anytime," she says quasi-apologetically.

Fatima's uneasiness dates back to the time she was waiting for resettlement, when she was reluctant to come to the United States. She gets emotional remembering that time and says frankly, "To be honest, before I came, I didn't like the US, the people, because of the war, because of what happened." What happened was the US invasion of Iraq in 2003, which left Fatima with a negative impression of Americans. She continues, "What you see in the news on TV is different to what you see here. What I saw there, they just came from a different country to kill our people, and to take what we have. I thought all American people are the army."

When Fatima came to the United States, the stereotype she had about Americans collapsed. First, she realized that "people here don't know anything about Iraq, about Middle East, so it is not about people; it is politics." Also, Americans were downright kind to her. Fatima says, "Maybe I was lucky because I met the right people, but it just changed my mind. They were very nice and they didn't stare at me because of the way I look or because I have accent." "The way I look" refers to the way Fatima dresses, chiefly that she wears a headscarf, and she expects Americans to treat her differently because of it. She recalls, "When I had my first baby, she was premature, so she stayed in the incubator for a month. The nurses saw I wear hijab, I am covering my hair, but they were very nice to my daughter and me. They really took care of my daughter, even though I am different, like, I don't look the same."

Although Fatima has been pleasantly surprised by her encounters with Americans, she still retains an air of self-consciousness, and she does sense resistance to her hijab at times: "Until now, it happens. I feel it is a barrier." She admits that she has not experienced animosity herself but has heard "so many stories" of women not getting promoted at work or of students being mocked at school and college. Fatima muses, "I don't know. It's complicated. It's challenging. I was thinking about it just this morning: maybe things would be so much easier if I am not wearing hijab. I could have so many other opportunities." However, this is something that Fatima is determined not to change about herself. "I can take it off but I don't like to. It is who I am; I believe in it. I didn't come here to change my personality, to change who I am. I just came here to live a peaceful life."

ISLAND OF ISOLATION

Who I am: ultimately, it is a question of identity and belonging, one that Faisal is grappling with right now. "For me, it's always a debate, a negotiation going on inside my mind, questioning my identity: Who am I? Where do I belong?"

Faisal's questions are born of sadness and frustration. He comes from Afghanistan and moved to the United States in 2016, only to feel that both home and host country have let him down badly. Faisal belongs to the marginalized Hazara group, so he has seen plenty of injustice in his life of forty-odd years. A fiercely proud man, he veers toward rejecting his country because of it. "I hate to say this, but I hate Afghanistan, because I never felt it is my country." But he admits to nostalgia too: "Still, my parents are there; it is where my personality started building, where I fell in love, where I made friends."

Faisal's bitterness at his homeland is understandable, because of discrimination against the Hazara, which was "so normalized in our country," and because of the endless wars. He became a refugee at the age of ten, moving to Pakistan with his family. Life was very hard. Together with his two younger sisters, Faisal spent most of his time weaving carpets with his bare hands to support the family. After years in exile, the family returned to Afghanistan in 2001 when an international coalition defeated the Taliban. Faisal remembers, "My father was so excited; he could not even stay for one more day in Pakistan. The very next day after hearing the news, he left."

Back in Afghanistan, Faisal did well in school and went on to study management and administration. Although he topped his class, he was passed over for an important job when he graduated, an experience that he describes as "so funny and so painful" and that he attributes to ethnic discrimination and corruption. The job he wanted was one of two hundred positions available with a national agency. He says, "The funny thing was that two of my classmates, who I used to help with their studies because they didn't speak good English, were hired. One said he knew a politician and the other said his father's friend was working there."

Badly disappointed, Faisal decided to go to university, and then he took some time out to work as an interpreter with the US military so he could pay his tuition fees. He was deployed to Helmand Province, which he describes as "hell, one of the worst provinces, and still is." He gives a wry laugh: "College boy going directly to Special Forces. It was a rough time, scary. I learned a lot." His voice is not without pride as he remembers, "You go on real live mission, to the battlefield. We went to the regions where the Taliban are, the red zones, and came back. We had targets; it was real operations." After nine months, Faisal resigned and returned to school, carrying an "amazing" reference that made good all his sacrifices.

Back in Kabul, Faisal returned to work with the US Army while continuing his studies. Although he was based in the city with training teams, it was not as if he was safe. He says, "Sometimes I felt safer on the battlefield than in the city because Kabul has a lot of suicide attacks." Once, Faisal remembers, he was in a van taxi when suddenly there was a "boom, a huge tremor, a huge shock." They had just missed a bomb blast. "Believe it or not, there was only a minute of difference. God saved me. In Kabul, you don't know when. You sometimes see things that really shock you."

Faisal migrated to San Diego with a Special Immigrant Visa (SIV), which is granted to Afghans who worked for the US government. Over seventy-nine thousand individuals were granted this visa by the end of 2018 under three SIV programs for Iraqi and Afghan nationals, including the applicants and their families. While Iraqis may no longer apply, more than seventeen thousand Afghans who have applied over the years are still waiting to find out whether they will be accepted. The process can take years of nail-biting frustration, during which time the applicants fear reprisal daily because they worked for or on behalf of the United States. Delays are put down to limited visa availability, bureaucratic bottlenecks, and rigorous security screening, which has become even more extreme in recent years.

The hard-won opportunity did not translate into happiness for Faisal. He puts his malaise down to "my own isolation." As Faisal describes it, however, the crippling sense of loneliness is not his alone; he believes that "every refugee in this country has his own island of isolation." Faisal vests the word with a unique meaning. "Isolation does not mean that you don't speak to people. Being a refugee, you leave behind your identity, your job, your social status, your family, whatever you built during your life, your memories, your childhood, the places you love to go to eat, drink, and walk. Then you go to a new life and the most painful thing is when you don't feel welcome in the society."

Faisal counted on finding his place in the United States. He had high expectations because he had already lost so much in his life and because, as he acknowledges, "we have this narrative in our hand of what we did for you." Faisal is referring to the time he spent working for the US military in Afghanistan. He elaborates, "We saved lives of US soldiers on mission. If you translate a piece of information that an IED [improvised explosive device] is here, and somebody does not go that way, that means saved, right?" Faisal put his life on the line to do this job: "Every moment, you predict your death . . . yeah, we've been through that." Faisal also mentions the stigma he suffered among his own people, and the predictable death threats from the Taliban, because he worked for the US military.

When Faisal came to the United States with his wife, it was the racist remark of a total stranger that exposed the fragility of his hopes for a new life. It happened in a parking lot, when Faisal was first in a row of cars waiting to leave via a one-way exit. The road had been blocked following an accident, and a woman wanted to drive into the parking lot the wrong way but could not do so. Since Faisal's was the first car, she vented her road rage on him: "When her car passed mine, she rolled down the window, spat at me, and swore. She told me, 'F°°°ing chong-chong,' because she thought I was Chinese." That did it for Faisal. "This really broke my castle, which I had made in my mind out of the US, out of this new life. I am not, in the lady's words, a 'f°°°ing chong-chong.' I just worked with your military, but nobody understands in this society." Faisal gets so upset when he remembers this distasteful encounter that tears of frustration appear. "The dream I had of America was broken, and it's very hard to fix it. It probably takes another life to build."

Faisal feels betrayed and is disinclined to give second chances, saying he can no longer trust anyone. "I lost thirty years in war and conflicts, violence and a fearful environment. Here, it is painful and disappointing when I have the things I wanted—security, a stable life, a country with peace—but I am just struggling with integration." This is the chill of Faisal's isolation. Let down by both home and host countries, he is still desperately trying to work things out in his mind. He calls it "the weight of being a refugee: all the anxiety and stress, the conflict with yourself about your identity."

STARTING FROM ZERO

Disappointed expectation sits heavily on another SIV holder I meet in San Diego named Taqi. There is no stopping Taqi once he starts talking. He keeps thinking of another point he needs to make, another anecdote he needs to tell, to get things off his chest. "I worked with the US Army in Afghanistan, at a big gas station. I am an engineer," he says by way of introducing himself. "After that, I got some threats, because I worked for the US Army. They sent a message that 'We will kill you, and kidnap your kids,' and so I applied to come here. I think when we came in US, everything will be good, but unfortunately living in US is also too difficult for us."

Taqi has been in the United States since 2017. The hardest thing is starting "from zero" to find a job, a place to live, a place in society, and "I have to start from zero in my knowledge also." This is what bothers Taqi most of all. He says, "I have fifteen years' experience working in oil and gas but I couldn't find a good job to fit my experience here, just a job at a warehouse." Taqi is upset not only because he could find no better than an entry-level job, but also because his dreams of doing further studies have been dashed, at least for now. "When I came here, it was in my mind to improve my knowledge, to go to university to get a master's, to try to find a good position. But now I am here, I am working, and I think I can't do it," he says. There is no way that Taqi can afford to study at the moment. He is busy providing for his wife, who does not work, and for their three children, ages five to twelve.

Paying rent is probably his biggest headache, for a small apartment "in a block with thirteen families from different places." Taqi has nostalgic memories of his roomy house in Afghanistan, which he owned and did not need to pay a penny for. His former home is not all that Taqi hankers after. "We miss our family: father, mother, brother, everyone we miss." Taqi has lots of sympathy for his wife: "She stays crying; she misses her mum. For the ladies, it is too difficult. For us, we go outside, we talk with each other, as friends, but they are all the time sitting at home."

Taqi sighs throughout our conversation, which is punctuated with his oft-repeated admission that "the US is very difficult for everything." The story that seems to matter most to him is about the first time the family went on a big shopping spree soon after arriving. They went to a Walmart to buy the basics and piled bags of purchases into the shopping cart. Then the cart stalled. Taqi had no idea why. He changed carts but the same thing happened. Taqi did not know anything about taxi apps or public transport. He distributed the bags among his family and they started walking home, but still his own load was too heavy. Taqi was upset because it was the first time he had asked his wife to carry something herself. "In my country, I would have just called a taxi, but here I didn't know what to do," he says. As if almost embarrassed to admit it, he adds, "That day, I almost cried. I tried to go back home." He bounced back soon enough and is conversant with life in the United States now, but that seemingly trivial incident is one Taqi will never forget.

Taqi is not steeped in unremitting gloom and pessimism. He has a great sense of humor, which sparkles through the stories of stress, and he tries to find the positive side in things. About missing relatives back home, he says, "Now we can talk to our family on the phone all the time. We can call, and we see each other on video. That's a good point." He grins and tells an anecdote by way of comparison. "In 2000, I was at university in Afghanistan but far from my house, some ten hours' travel, and we had no phone. I would write a letter to say I am OK. Months later, when I went home to visit, my letter would arrive two or three days after me. I'd say to my parents, 'Oh, I am here myself now, so you can see I am OK.'"

Taqi also finds comic absurdity in the way life in the United States is so different from life in Afghanistan, for better or for worse. He finds Americans kind and has made friends, but he laments the fact that everyone is so busy that you need to make an appointment just to speak to any of them. Bureaucracy in hospitals is another bugbear. "They give you a lot of papers to fill in, but you don't know some words, like jargon, and there is no one to explain," he says in exasperation. "You have to write 'yes' or 'no,' and I don't know which is right. I write all of them 'no.' Perhaps I have those health problems, but anyway I write 'no.'"

Ultimately, like Waleed and Fatima, Taqi is ambivalent about the opportunity to live in America. He might find it very hard, as does his wife, but he also appreciates the security and the fact that his kids are happy. Is Taqi hopeful about his family's future in the United States? "It's so-so," he replies thoughtfully. "We came here. We have to live here. That's the choice. Life is going on, anywhere you are, but I am thinking about my kids. They are happy." He still hopes "to find a good house and to study" and that things will get better with time. But the passing of time is another anxiety for Taqi. His expressive face breaks into a grin again: "I lose everything. My hair was black but now . . . and I had a good face but now . . ." He points to some gray hairs and fine wrinkles.

At the end of our chat, I take leave of Taqi hoping that he'll have the last laugh, and that he'll manage to go back to school, to get a better job, and to move into a house with his family. Somehow, I think he will. His disposition promises to take him a long way, and statistics about the integration of refugees in the United States are in his favor, indicating that their initial struggles pay off and that they progress economically in a relatively short time.

23

"THERE IS ALWAYS ANOTHER CHANCE"

A WHOLE NEW WORLD

Not all have their expectations disappointed. Layla says, "America is how I expected it to be—it helped me when I needed help. People are very good here. In every country, you find people who are good and people who are bad." Apart from feeling safe, Layla is glad that her five children "have opportunities here for learning that we couldn't have in our country, so we are making our way."

Layla herself admits to being lonely but plans to start going to community college to improve her English. She spends most of her time at home. "Home" is a small house on a wide street in San Diego, with lovely hill views all around and a garden with a bizarrely tall palm tree. When I visit, she is effusive in her welcome, especially because I go with Kathryn, an American woman who volunteers with a resettlement agency and who taught Layla English when she first arrived. Layla brings a tray of fragrant coffee and Iraqi pastries and willingly talks about herself.

Layla's family left their homeland of Iraq after her husband narrowly escaped an assassination attempt. A high-ranking official in the Iraqi army, he also helped its American counterpart as an interpreter and decided to apply for an SIV to migrate to the United States. Eventually, the entire family got there, but it was not plain sailing. First, Layla's husband, daughter, and one son went, followed by the two eldest sons, and finally Layla herself arrived with her youngest son.

Layla's twelve-year-old daughter is sitting in the living room with us. Dalal is translating for her mum but is bursting to tell her part of the story too. When her mother talks about the time the family was separated, Dalal pipes up: "It was really hard. I couldn't see my mum for six months. I was only ten years old. It was Ramadan when I left with my dad for the US. My mum fainted when we said bye."

Layla looks at Dalal with adoring and affectionate eyes and says, "I missed my daughter so much." She clasps her arms around herself in an empty hug. Dalal continues talking quickly and earnestly: "I had just graduated from fourth grade and I had to go to a whole new world, without my mother and without anything, and with zero English. I had only just started learning how to read and write in Arabic and now I had to learn English and the people around me were speaking Spanish." When Dalal left Iraq for the United States with her dad, they went to Atlanta, Georgia, first, to a place with a large Hispanic community. Dalal was homesick and bullied at school because she wore a hijab. Other students used to tell her, "Why do you wear that? You look ugly."

Dalal's experience is far from unique. Fatima works with young refugees and she says many confide in her about bullying, especially in middle school. "The students have so many things going on. I hear so many stories about people making fun of them because of the way they look, because of the way they talk." When I ask who the culprits are, she points a finger at "some students, sometimes the teachers." It appears to be diversity that prompts the bullying. Fatima explains: "The language, and the way the students look, it's totally different. Like, people from Afghanistan, the others make fun of the way they dress: 'Why are you dressing like this? Are you going to a party?' It hurts them, even if they laugh about it. They want to be normal kids. They don't want to be different; they want to be the same as the others."

School had one saving grace for Dalal: "The only good thing was my teacher. She was nice and she helped me, unlike the girls. I started learning English and I actually love the language." Dalal runs to her room to get her laptop, to show us an essay she wrote about Iraq. She writes about the family house in Baghdad, "big and white, with golden-colored gates that looked fashionable and kind of expensive."

Dalal was overjoyed when her mother and brothers finally joined them in the United States. But they brought news that broke her heart. "I lost my pet, a husky," she says, bursting into tears before she even finishes the sentence. "He was the best friend ever, for me. We really loved Brown." Her pet was killed after Dalal left Baghdad, when her brother inadvertently left the door of the house open because he was late for a football game. "Brown loved going out, so he ran out and some people tried to steal him. They did not manage to catch him so they shot him instead," Dalal says tearfully. She explains that it was common for handsome dogs like Brown to be stolen by "dog hunters" in Baghdad, which was why they never let him free. Brown crawled back to the doorstep and they found him bleeding there. He died of his injuries after several days. Dalal and her brother show us photos of Brown, alive in good health, dying, and dead.

Dalal's life took a turn for the better when the family moved to San Diego, where she likes school because she has made Arab friends. There is a thriving community of Iraqis and Syrians in the neighborhood to which they moved. "We knew our people were here," she says. Dalal ends her essay with words fitting for these pages: "In my personal experience, the only message I want to give to all my readers is that: Even though you feel like you've lost hope, know that there is always another chance."

A RICHLY DESERVED F

Since the passage of the Refugee Act in 1980 with massive bipartisan support, the United States has given another chance to nearly three million refugees under the Refugee Admissions Program. But numbers have sunk to unprecedented lows in recent years, from nearly 85,000 in 2016 to less than 22,500 in 2018. The president sets the ceiling for refugee admissions every year in consultation with Congress. During his first weeks in office, President Donald Trump suspended the refugee resettlement program for 120 days by executive order. Then he brought the refugee admission ceiling crashing down. Things went downhill from there and, for 2019, the ceiling was set at a meager thirty thousand, the lowest since the program began nearly forty years ago. Due to increased security vetting for refugees, actual admissions fell even lower than the ceilings. In 2018, the ceiling was forty-five thousand, but only half that number actually arrived in the United States.

The figures speak for themselves. Underlying the policy shift is a narrative that inaccurately and unfairly links refugees with terrorism and crime. Trump has repeatedly demonized refugees, especially those arriving from Muslim countries, both as president and during his campaign to gain that office. Translating invective into policy meant more security vetting for refugees, on the grounds that it was insufficient before and that the entire admission program was faulty. These claims are dismissed as utterly mistaken by those who have worked in resettlement in the United States for years, and who can vouch that the admissions program so vilified by Trump *always* had a very thorough vetting process.

The rhetoric and policy decisions of the Trump administration have a very adverse impact on refugees both in the United States and abroad. Some of those already in the States, those who were working to bring their families to join them, have had their hopes crushed. Waleed is one of them. He applied to bring his mother and siblings from Iraq. "Four years have passed and nothing happened," he says. "The current political climate and administration, you know, they say they have new security measures. OK, that's it then, done." He guesses the process will come to nothing "because they literally put your file on the shelf."

Iraq is one of eleven countries that the administration has designated as "high risk." Others include Syria, South Sudan, Somalia, and Yemen. Only a handful of refugees from these countries were resettled to the United States in 2018, if at all. As Waleed says, "It doesn't make sense," but there you go. There are many examples of the way in which this administration has eroded the principles of compassion and justice in its approach to refugees and immigrants. Its hostility toward the resettlement program is just one. No wonder Refugees International, an advocacy NGO, gave the Trump administration a richly deserved F for its refugee policy.

WELCOME TO AMERICA

Happily, many Americans still strongly support the idea of a just and generous refugee policy. As soon as Trump announced the infamous travel bans in early 2017, people across the country responded to the negative political climate with increased offers of financial donations, volunteer engagement, and more.

Volunteers teaching English to newly arrived refugees with the re-settlement agency in San Diego reveal this side of America. Jennifer, who has been involved for ten years, says, "I feel like it's really impor-tant to do something, whatever little ripple you can cause . . . that helps us cope with what's going on." Jennifer is referring to the political climate. However, she finds her voluntary work to be invaluable for her own sake too. "You can easily get caught in your own little bubble in life and never really come out, so it's one of these things I do to broaden my life," says Jennifer. "I feel I have a blessed and secure life and this helps me balance it."

Another volunteer, Karen, loves the feeling of welcoming people to America given the "who-knows-what circumstances they've come out of, very difficult situations. I just love the sense of community that I am part of sharing and giving to them." Something Karen has learned is that there is no typical profile of a refugee: "Before, I did one-on-one tutorship with immigrants and refugees arriving in the US. I started with a group of people who had never seen a pencil. And then one of my first classes out here was a group of Iraqis, all of whom were engi-neers, lawyers, doctors, teachers. So the whole range."

The volunteers have huge empathy for the refugees. Karen contin-ues, "We don't know, because we've not experienced, what they've been through. They come here and there must be some real trepidation on their part. Yet they come in every day with a smile, hug, or hand-shake. We laugh together, and find joy in each class, and get some business done."

There is also the desire to reach out across manmade boundaries. Another volunteer, Kathryn, has been moved by the depth of the rela-tionships she has formed with the refugees. To sum up her feelings about them, Kathryn borrows a line from the musical *Wicked*: "You'll be with me like a handprint on my heart."

24

DO UNTO OTHERS . . .

Refugees do not leave their country because they want to, but because they are forced to do so. They leave in search of life—"not a better life, just life," as one Syrian told me firmly. In a bitter irony, many die in their bid to find life because they are not allowed to travel through "legal pathways," in humanitarian jargon. Without documentation to gain entry to the territory where they might seek asylum, they are forced to play Russian roulette, with the chances of survival as low as one in fourteen. That itself should be an indication of their despair.

But despair is not enough to convince policymakers that people need protection from whatever it is they are running away from. Many refugees are not accepted as such. The narrow and inexpert application of refugee definitions dismisses many applicants who in fact deserve protection from life-threatening violence in all its forms, including its insidious cultural and structural manifestations.

Being defined as a refugee is critically important for people who need protection because this status confers essential rights and benefits. At the same time, this word can be a double-edged sword, because it is also used as a label that sits ill with many who are thus categorized. Like the rest of us, refugees are human beings first and foremost, and they do not want socially ascribed labels to obscure their identity. But in a world where the rhetoric of populist politicians resonates with sizable segments of voters around the world, refugees and migrants are relentlessly stereotyped and scapegoated.

The global picture is depressing. On the one hand, there is no letup
in the crises fueling flows of refugees; on the other hand, the popular
tide seems to be turning against welcoming them. While I was writing
this book, I faced the same challenges as those who shared their stories
with me: How could I find the language to do justice to what I heard,
without resorting to the same overtired words and clichés? In how
many different ways can you effectively describe things that are beyond
bearing: despair, fear, brutality, a traumatic past, and a hostile reception?

But there were other sensations and actions that I was hard pressed
to put into words, and they epitomize a counter-witness to a world that
at once creates and rejects refugees. I will borrow two biblical refer-
ences to explain what I mean. In this book, I designated some individuals who helped the refugees on the road as Good Samaritans. So many
are featured in the stories. Some are mentioned only in passing, like the
residents of Melilla and Marseille who generously responded to refugees' pleas for some change to buy food, or the tourist in Morocco who
gave his own clothes and shoes. Others, I had no space to mention, like
people from Bosnia who pressed money, clothes, shoes, and food on the
refugees they passed in the street. These Good Samaritans came from
everywhere and the refugees themselves feature among them as much
as anyone else.

The comparison with the Good Samaritan, the mythical protagonist
of one of the parables of Jesus, is apt because he helped a wounded
traveler who came from a group different than his own. This willingness
to help others in need, whoever they may be, characterized the people
of goodwill I heard about and met. The members of the Welcome
Network in Marseille all had the same answer ready when I asked them
why they invite asylum seekers to stay with them. First, they said, "Because they are human beings." And then, another leaf from the book of
Jesus, they proclaimed the Golden Rule: "Do unto others as you would
have them do unto you" (Matthew 7:12). No great explanations needed.
In San Diego, the volunteers displayed solid empathy for refugees, not
for what they *knew* they had passed through (often they didn't know),
but for what they *imagined* the experience must have been. They
trusted that the refugees had a compelling reason to leave their country.

Tragically, our world is trending toward the criminalization of solidarity with refugees and migrants. Data compiled by the global media

platform Open Democracy reveals that more than 250 Europeans have been arrested, investigated, and/or charged in court over the past five years for providing food, shelter, transport, or other support to migrants. Those targeted include a priest nominated for the Nobel Peace Prize, a football player, firefighters, farmers, ex-soldiers, pensioners, and many local politicians. Such intimidation is on the rise.

The signs are ominous, not least because we already have a repugnant historical precedent for this. A Polish friend tells a story about his grandparents, who lived in Nazi-occupied Poland in World War II. Once, grandmother enraged grandfather because she gave a loaf of bread to a Jewish woman who came begging with her children. Grandfather was furious because he was terrified that the spontaneous act of compassion had put the entire family in mortal danger.

Not only do we fail to grasp the hallowed lessons of history, to our peril, but we are also slow to learn from what is happening in the here and now. In 2015, a photo of the lifeless body of three-year-old Alan Kurdi, washed up on a Turkish beach, sparked an international outcry. Kurdi was a Syrian boy who drowned in the Mediterranean Sea after the boat carrying his family and other refugees sank. Today, how many children and their parents die in the same sea while rescue vessels are prevented from saving them?

One of the young men I interviewed, who is recognized as a refugee and getting on happily with his life, wanted to say one more thing when I switched off the recorder. The first time he tried to cross the sea, with his mother and younger brother and sister, the boat sank. He was the only one to survive and he was powerless to save them. He was in the sea for fourteen hours before he was rescued and sent back home. "You see, I suffered a lot to get here," he said through his tears. My friend shared this part of his story, which he usually keeps private, because he believes that if people out there know about such stories, they will act to ensure they never happen again.

His belief in a universal push for change was spurred by the outpouring of sorrow at Kurdi's death. For him, that reaction meant people cared for his story, too, and this was a solace. I silently dissented from his view that the revelation of similar tragedies will make a discernable difference, but I want his unspoken appeal to be the last word. He is convinced that change will come from listening to the stories of refugees. Don't let him down.

ACRONYMS

CETI   Centro de Estancia Temporal de Inmigrantes (Center for Temporary Stay for Immigrants), Melilla, Spain

EU   European Union

FGM   female genital mutilation

FSA   Free Syrian Army

IED   improvised explosive device

IRC   International Rescue Committee

JRS   Jesuit Refugee Service

NGO   nongovernmental organization

SIV   Special Immigrant Visa

SPLA   Sudan People's Liberation Army

UN   United Nations

UNHCR United Nations High Commissioner for Refugees

REFERENCES

Airwars. "US-led Coalition in Iraq and Syria: Estimates of Civilian Deaths." https://airwars. org/conflict/coalition-in-iraq-and-syria.

Alvarez, Priscilla. "'How Much More Merit Do You Need Than Saving American Lives?'" *The Atlantic,* July 25, 2018. https://www.theatlantic.com/politics/archive/2018/07/trump-immigration-crackdown-visas/565949.

Asylum Information Database (AIDA) and European Council on Refugees and Exiles (ECRE). "Access to the Territory and Pushbacks: Spain." http://www.asylumineurope.org/ reports/country/spain/access-territory-and-push-backs.

———. *Refugee Rights Subsiding? Europe's Two-Tier Protection Regime and Its Effect on the Rights of Beneficiaries.* 2016. https://www.refworld.org/docid/58e1fc8e4.html.

———. "Statistics: France." https://www.asylumineurope.org/reports/country/france/ statistics.

Boukhars, Anouar. "Barriers versus Smugglers: Algeria and Morocco's Battle for Border Security." Carnegie Endowment for International Peace, March 19, 2019. https:// carnegieendowment.org/2019/03/19/barriers-versus-smugglers-algeria-and-morocco-s-battle-for-border-security-pub-78618.

British and Irish Agencies Afghanistan Group (BAAG) and European Network of NGOs in Afghanistan (ENNA). "Return and Displacement in Afghanistan" (discussion paper). March 2018. https://www.ecoi.net/en/file/local/1430450/1226_1524550555_return-and-displacement-in-afghanistan-march-2018.pdf.

Bruno, Andorra. *Iraqi and Afghan Special Immigrant Visa Programs.* Congressional Research Service, Report R43725. Updated March 29, 2019. https://fas.org/sgp/crs/homesec/ R43725.pdf.

Campbell, Zach. "Spain's Civilian Coast Guard Caught in Election Crosshairs." Politico, September 25, 2019. https://www.politico.eu/article/spain-migration-civilian-coast-guard-caught-in-election-crosshairs.

Capps, Randy, and Michael Fix. *Ten Facts about U.S. Refugee Resettlement.* Migration Policy Institute (MPI). October 2015. https://www.migrationpolicy.org/research/ten-facts-about-us-refugee-resettlement.

Child Soldiers International. "Child Soldier Levels Doubled Since 2012 and Girls' Exploitation Is Rising." February 11, 2019. https://www.child-soldiers.org/news/child-soldier-levels-have-doubled-since-2012-and-girls-exploitation-is-rising.

European Asylum Support Office (EASO). "Latest Asylum Trends—2018 Overview." February 13, 2019. https://www.easo.europa.eu/asylum-trends-overview-2018.

European Council. "EU-Turkey Statement." March 18, 2016. https://www.consilium.europa. eu/en/press/press-releases/2016/03/18/eu-turkey-statement.

Eurostat. "EU Member States Granted Protection to More Than 300,000 Asylum Seekers in 2018." April 25, 2019.

Eurostat, Statistics Explained. *Asylum Quarterly Report*. March 12, 2019.

Francois, Myriam. "The Moroccan Fishmonger Who Broke the Camel's Back." *Middle East Eye*, November 1, 2016. https://www.middleeasteye.net/opinion/moroccan-fishmonger-who-broke-camels-back.

Gier, Nicholas F. "The Genocide of the Hazaras: Descendants of Genghis Khan Fight for Survival in Afghanistan and Pakistan." Revised and expanded version of keynote address, annual meeting of the American Mongol Association, November 8, 2014.

Global Coalition to Protect Education from Attack (GCPEA). *Education under Attack*. 2018. http://eua2018.protectingeducation.org.

Hanlon, Querine, and Matthew M. Herbert. *Border Security Challenges in the Grand Maghreb*. Peaceworks no. 109, United States Institute for Peace (USIP). 2015.

Hayden, Sally. "The EU's Deal with Libya Is Sentencing Refugees to Death." *The Guardian*, February 5, 2019. https://www.theguardian.com/commentisfree/2019/feb/05/eu-deal-libya-refugees-libyan-detention-centres.

Human Rights Watch (HRW). *Eritrea and Ethiopia. The Horn of Africa War: Mass Expulsions and the Nationality Issue (June 1998—April 2002)*. Vol. 15, no. 3 (A) (January 2003). https://www.hrw.org/reports/2003/ethioerit0103/ethioerit0103.pdf.

———. "EU/Italy/Libya: Disputes over Rescues Put Lives at Risk." July 25, 2018. https://www.hrw.org/news/2018/07/25/eu/italy/libya-disputes-over-rescues-put-lives-risk.

———. *"I Wanted to Lie Down and Die." Trafficking and Torture of Eritreans in Sudan and Egypt*. February 11, 2014. https://www.hrw.org/report/2014/02/11/i-wanted-lie-down-and-die/trafficking-and-torture-eritreans-sudan-and-egypt#page.

———. *No Escape from Hell: EU Policies Contribute to Abuse of Migrants in Libya*. January 21, 2019. https://www.hrw.org/report/2019/01/21/no-escape-hell/eu-policies-contribute-abuse-migrants-libya.

———. *Off the Radar: Human Rights in the Tindouf Refugee Camps*. October 18, 2014. https://www.hrw.org/report/2014/10/18/radar/human-rights-tindouf-refugee-camps.

———. *Pakistan Coercion, UN Complicity: The Mass Forced Return of Afghan Refugees*. February 13, 2017. https://www.hrw.org/report/2017/02/13/pakistan-coercion-un-complicity/mass-forced-return-afghan-refugees.

———. *World Report 2019: Eritrea, Events of 2018*. https://www.hrw.org/world-report/2019/country-chapters/eritrea.

———. *World Report 2019: Morocco/Western Sahara, Events of 2018*. https://www.hrw.org/world-report/2019/country-chapters/morocco/western-sahara.

Ijaz, Saroop. "Pakistan's Scapegoating of Afghans." *Express Tribune*, November 19, 2015. https://tribune.com.pk/story/994087/pakistans-scapegoating-of-afghans.

Imhof, Oliver. "Four Years of War and ISIS Is Almost Defeated—But at What Cost?" Airwars, August 8, 2018. https://airwars.org/news-and-investigations/four-years-of-war-and-isis-is-almost-defeated-but-at-what-cost.

International Crisis Group. *Salvaging South Sudan's Fragile Peace Deal*. Africa Report no. 270. March 13, 2019. https://www.crisisgroup.org/africa/horn-africa/south-sudan/270-salvaging-south-sudans-fragile-peace-deal.

International Organization for Migration (IOM), Global Migration Data Analysis Centre. *The Central Mediterranean Route: Migrant Fatalities, January 2014–July 2017*. August 2018. https://gmdac.iom.int/the-central-mediterranean-route-migrant-fatalities-january-july-2017.

Kadi, Samar. "Lebanon's Youth Bearing the Brunt of Unemployment, Regional Instability." *Arab Weekly*, August 6, 2017. https://thearabweekly.com/lebanons-youth-bearing-brunt-unemployment-regional-instability.

Lebanese Republic, Presidency of the Council of Ministers, Central Administration of Statistics. "Key Indicators." http://www.cas.gov.lb/index.php/86-english/key-indicators-en.

Nabert, Alexander, Claudia Torrisi, Nandini Archer, Belen Lobos, and Claire Provost. "Hundreds of Europeans 'Criminalised' for Helping Migrants—As Far Right Aims to Win Big in European Elections." *Open Democracy*, May 18, 2019. https://www.opendemocracy.

net/en/5050/hundreds-of-europeans-criminalised-for-helping-migrants-new-data-shows-as-far-right-aims-to-win-big-in-european-elections.

Najib. "Unemployment Rate in Lebanon at 46%?" *Blogbaladi*, March 30, 2018. https://blogbaladi.com/unemployment-rate-in-lebanon-at-46.

Niarchos, Nicolas. "Is One of Africa's Oldest Conflicts Finally Nearing Its End?" *New Yorker*, December 29, 2018. https://www.newyorker.com/news/news-desk/is-one-of-africas-oldest-conflicts-finally-nearing-its-end.

Operation Inherent Resolve. "Combined Joint Task Force—Operation Inherent Resolve Monthly Civilian Casualty Report." September 26, 2019. https://www.inherentresolve.mil/Media-Library/News-Releases/Article/1971680/combined-joint-task-force-operation-inherent-resolve-monthly-civilian-casualty.

Parusel, Bernd. "Afghan Asylum Seekers and the Deficits of the Common European Asylum System." *FlüchtlingsforschungsBlog*, February 19, 2018. https://fluechtlingsforschung.net/afghan-asylum-seekers-deficits-common-european-asylum-system.

Pierce, Sarah. *Immigration-Related Policy Changes in the First Two Years of the Trump Administration*. Migration Policy Institute (MPI). May 2019. https://www.migrationpolicy.org/research/immigration-policy-changes-two-years-trump-administration.

Pontifical Council "Cor Unum" and Pontifical Council for the Pastoral Care of Migrants and Itinerant People. *Refugees: A Challenge to Solidarity*. 1992. http://www.vatican.va/roman_curia/pontifical_councils/corunum/documents/rc_pc_corunum_doc_25061992_refugees_en.html.

Refugees International. *Report Card: The Trump Administration's Performance on Refugee and Humanitarian Protection*. June 20, 2018. https://www.refugeesinternational.org/reports/2018/6/19/report-card-on-the-trump-administrations-performance-on-refugee-and-humanitarian-protection.

Taylor, Diane. "Most Refugees in Libyan Detention Centres at Risk—UN." *The Guardian*, May 31, 2019. https://www.theguardian.com/world/2019/may/31/un-calls-for-evacuation-of-libyan-refugees-amid-dire-conditions.

Tondo, Lorenzo. "Italian Authorities Order Seizure of Migrant Rescue Ship." *The Guardian*, March 20, 2019. https://www.theguardian.com/world/2019/mar/20/italian-authorities-order-seizure-migrant-rescue-ship-mare-jonio.

UN News. "South Sudan: 'Outraged' UN Experts Say Ongoing Widespread Human Rights Violations May Amount to War Crimes." February 20, 2019. https://news.un.org/en/story/2019/02/1033181.

United Nations Assistance Mission in Afghanistan (UNAMA), Human Rights Service. *2018 Annual Report on the Protection of Civilians in Armed Conflict in Afghanistan*. February 2019. https://unama.unmissions.org/sites/default/files/unama_annual_protection_of_civilians_report_2018_-_23_feb_2019_-_english.pdf.

United Nations Children's Fund (UNICEF). *A Deadly Journey for Children: The Central Mediterranean Migration Route*. Child Alert series. February 2017. https://www.unicef.org/publications/index_94905.html.

United Nations Children's Fund (UNICEF), United Nations High Commissioner for Refugees (UNHCR), and United Nations World Food Programme (WFP). *Vulnerability Assessment for Syrian Refugees in Lebanon (VASyR-2018)*. December 2018. https://www.unhcr.org/lb/wp-content/uploads/sites/16/2018/12/VASyR-2018.pdf.

United Nations High Commissioner for Refugees (UNHCR). *Desperate Journeys: Refugees and Migrants Arriving in Europe and at Europe's Borders, January–December 2018*. January 2019. https://www.unhcr.org/desperatejourneys.

———. *Global Trends: Forced Displacement in 2018*. June 19, 2019. https://www.unhcr.org/globaltrends2018.

———. *Refugees and Migrants: Arrivals to Europe in 2018 (Mediterranean)*. 2019. https://data2.unhcr.org/en/documents/download/68006.

United Nations Human Rights Council. *Report of the Independent International Commission of Inquiry on the Syrian Arab Republic*. January 31, 2019.

United Nations Human Rights Council, Independent International Commission of Inquiry on the Syrian Arab Republic. *Rule of Terror: Living under ISIS in Syria.* November 14, 2014.

United States Department of State. *Trafficking in Persons Report.* June 2019. https://www.state.gov/wp-content/uploads/2019/06/2019-Trafficking-in-Persons-Report.pdf.

Viscusi, Gregory. "Macron Says EU Must Share Refugees, Expel Economic Migrants." *Bloomberg,* June 23, 2018. https://www.bloomberg.com/news/articles/2018-06-23/macron-says-eu-must-share-refugees-but-expel-economic-migrants.

Wintour, Patrick. "UN Calls for Inquiry into Libya Detention Centre Bombing." *The Guardian*, July 3, 2019. https://www.theguardian.com/world/2019/jul/03/air-strike-kill-libya-tripoli-migrant-detention-centre.

Yahya, Maha. "What Will It Take for Syrian Refugees to Return Home?" *Foreign Affairs*, May 28, 2018. https://www.foreignaffairs.com/articles/syria/2018-05-28/what-will-it-take-syrian-refugees-return-home.

INDEX

abduction, 9, 24; of children, 29–30; fear of, 35

abortion, 67

abuses, 37, 55; at borders, 11, 94; of human rights, 11; Libya and, 56

activists, 16; convictions of, 16; danger for, 155

Afghanistan, 11; Afghans and, 100–102; deportation to, 101; ISIS in, 10; Kabul in, 3, 101, 165; refugees from, 93, 104, 105; Taliban in, 7, 91

Africa Unita, 155

Airwars monitoring group, 37

Algeria, 77; Morocco and, 31, 85–86; Tindouf in, 30

arrest, 34, 56; activists and, 16; evasion of, 15

assassination attempts, 171

asylum, 5, 99; applications for, 148; Dublin Regulation and, 93; EU and, 100; expulsion and, 87; international law and, 62–63; rejection and, 145; request for, 79

bakery, 40

Balkan route, 94, 100

bandits, 56

beat, 92, 94, 95

beatings, 30, 54, 56, 86; Croatia and, 95; money and, 83; by police, 82

belonging, 161–169

boats, 57, 73, 74; as destination, 60, 61; drowning and, 4, 59; interception of, 62

Boko Haram, 82

bombs, 10, 36

borders, 86; abuses at, 11, 94; border management, 74; checkpoints at, 45, 50, 72; fences at, 77; the game at, 93; killings at, 98; smuggling and, 28; territory and, 72

branding, 29

Bright Future School, 13

Bulgaria, 91–92

burials, 46

Cameroon, 52, 81; Anglophone minority in, 81–82

Campo Sudan settlement, 17

capo, 52

captivity, 30; escape from, 77; money and, 83–84. *See also* enslavement

captors, 23

Carnegie, Dale, 127

La Carrera Africana ultramarathon, 88

Catania, 51, 62, 153, 155

Catholic Parish of James the Apostle, 73

Central Mediterranean route, 51; rescue missions and, 63; smugglers and traffickers on, 52

Centro de Estancia Temporal de Inmigrantes (CETI), 73; life at, 76, 78